ELAINE BELL KAPLAN

"We Live in the Shadow"

Inner-City Kids Tell Their Stories through Photographs

TEMPLE UNIVERSITY PRESS
PHILADELPHIA

TEMPLE UNIVERSITY PRESS
Philadelphia, Pennsylvania 19122
www.temple.edu/tempress

Library of Congress Cataloging-in-Publication Data

Kaplan, Elaine Bell.
   "We live in the shadow" : inner-city kids tell their stories
through photographs / Elaine Bell Kaplan.
      pages cm
   Includes bibliographical references and index.
   ISBN 978-1-4399-0789-4 (cloth : alk. paper) —
ISBN 978-1-4399-0790-0 (pbk. : alk. paper) —
ISBN 978-1-4399-0791-7 (e-book)   1. Inner cities—
United States.   2. City children—United States—Social
conditions.   3. Urban poor—United States—Social
conditions.   4. Equality—United States.
5. Photography—Social aspects—United States.   I. Title.
   HN59.2.K38 2013
   305—dc23
                                        2012042289

Printed in the United States of America

2 4 6 8 9 7 5 3 1

"We Live in the Shadow"

Photological Proof is not stringent, merely Overpowering

—Theodor W. Adorno, *The Culture Industry*

Contents

Acknowledgments

I owe a debt of gratitude to the brilliant kids who trusted me with their photos and stories and whose inner-city experiences challenge popular assumptions and theoretical perspectives about inner-city kids' lives. I give special thanks to the directors of the after-school centers who took time out of their busy schedules to talk with me and introduced me to the kids at the centers, especially Kim Thomas-Barrios, the director of the University of Southern California Neighborhood Academic Initiative (NAI), who granted me full access to the kids, their parents, and the extraordinary NAI staff, including Danielle Chavez and Angela Reyes. I owe a debt of gratitude to Isabel Duenes and Michelle Zavella, former NAI and USC graduates, who assisted in the early stages of this project with setting up interviews, typing transcripts, and sharing their views on the NAI program. This research could not have gotten off the ground as well as it did without their support and guidance. Gloria Sohacki introduced me to directors of several after-school progams. Her commitment to supporting the eduation and well-being of children serves as a model for me.

I was fortunate to have the support and many contributions of Karen Sternheimer, who had to sign off as coauthor because of her own writing commitments. She co-organized a workshop based on an earlier version of this book for the 2007 American Sociological Association annual meeting in New York City. And despite a busy schedule, she was always willing to lend me an ear when I rambled on about the kids in early-morning hallway meetings and to let her students attend a special class meeting to discuss an earlier version of this project. I offer a special thanks to Linda Fuller for her support and to Arlie Hochschild for offering critical analysis, insight, and encouragement in the early stages of this project and for her support throughout the years. Many drafts later, I remember having an "aha" moment when I discovered how much the theoretical perspective of the sociology of emotion added to my own take on the kids. Mitchell Duneier's powerful study of Greenwich Village street vendors, which included their interviews and photos, greatly aided my understanding of how to use the kids' photos and stories in a sociologically meaningful way.

I thank my colleagues Mike Messner and Pierrette Hondagneu-Sotelo for reading the first draft of half-baked ideas. I was sure they would throw the draft back at me. Instead, they took it seriously enough to critique my ideas and encourage me to move on. Other colleagues in my department offered me tremendous support, especially Veronica Terriquez and the former chair, Tim Biblarz, who suggested that I develop a visual sociology course based on the photovoice methodology used in this book. The sociology department provided funding for some expenses, and the current department chair, Rhacel Parrenas, was very supportive. Sharon Hays and Ed Ransford took time out of their busy schedules to read an early draft and told me to move ahead. Emir Loy, a former graduate student and my associate researcher, spent a great deal of time working with me at the NAI students' group meetings. Emir also created the certificate of participation given to the participants. Oscar Verdugo, a former undergraduate student, shared his experiences as a Latino teenager. Jeb Middlebrook was very supportive of this project, as were the students in my classes, who peppered me with comments and questions that contributed to my thinking about these issues. I also thank Stan Huey, whose knowledge of kids in gangs also added to my understanding of these kids. The great women of the sociology department's office staff, especially Lisa Rayburn, Stachelle Overland, Amber Thomas, and Melissa Hernandez, have all supported me in one way or another.

Special thanks go to Cynthia Hudley for reading a draft and for her keen analysis of the material and all her support throughout this long process, and to Manuel Pastor for taking time out of his busy day to talk with me. That talk led to another "aha" moment. I also learned much from the many conversations with the fantastic women in my Curves group, including Gloria Sohacki, Linda Poverny, and Kathy Yoshimi. I cannot say enough about Christine Cardone for the many insightful and stimulating conversations I had with her that greatly influenced my ideas about these kids. These women shared ideas, many of which I use in this book, as they pumped away on gym machines and when they viewed the photos at a potluck dinner.

I received a great deal of encouragement from Mick Gusinde-Duffy of Temple University Press, whose support of this project was important in getting to it to the final stages. I also thank Rebecca Logan at Newgen and other Temple staff who aided in the production of this work, including the anonymous reviewers for their valuable critiques.

My family has always been supportive of my work. My son, Daveed Franz Robert Kaplan, even offered to read the last draft. I thank him and Stephanie Kaplan for their support. I offer a special thanks to Shez Kennedy and Sherry Patterson and their kids and to Gloria and Selig Kaplan and Judy Kaplan for their interest in my work. I thank Lewis Kaplan, my soul mate, for his critical comments as he read draft after draft. I love his generosity of spirit, his deep compassion for these kids, his intellect and talent in understanding the way society works, and his commitment to changing the status quo. All these people have contributed to this book. I hope it meets their approval.

"We Live in the Shadow"

I

Kids with Cameras

Figure 1.1

1 |

"What Do You Want to Tell Me about This Picture?"[1]

On a bright spring day, ten middle schoolers from the Latino and African American communities in South Central Los Angeles,[1] ranging in age from twelve to fourteen, sit around an oval-shaped desk in a dimly lit second-floor classroom on the campus of the University of Southern California (USC) staring at a photograph of a railroad track (see Figure 1.1) featured on a PowerPoint slide. These middle schoolers are participating in the Neighborhood Academic Initiative (NAI) tutorial program sponsored by USC.[2] Twelve-year-old Cesar, who has taken the photo, waits a few minutes before he speaks up: "It's about that we can choose our path, the dark or the light; we can choose." Thirteen-year-old Manuel likes that idea: "Yeah, the tracks are a road to somewhere." Cesar shakes his head in agreement and says, "The tracks will get us away from the ghetto."

The other kids have a different view of the railroad track photograph. For thirteen-year-old Juan, "those tracks are in a dirty area." Fourteen-year-old Wynette agrees: "The railroad is in a bad environment." Six of the kids nod when thirteen-year-old Kyle adds, "It's ugly. That's what I see every day. . . . We live in the shadow, and no one sees that we are here." By the end of this two-year study, fifty-four kids have shared their experiences of living in the "ugly" South Central area. I also hold interviews with a smaller group consisting of twenty-one college students from USC, three teachers, two psychologists, the directors of NAI and the Willard Center, and fifteen

NAI parents—bringing the total to seventy-nine participants, all of whose perspectives I include in this book.[3]

Not every area of South Central can be considered ugly. But there are certain streets where the Bloods, the Crips, and the Mara Salvatrucha (M-13) gang dominate; where drive-by shootings occur regularly; and where drug dealers sell to school dropouts. In other words, South Central has a reputation as a community of kids that have little regard for law and order. Many kids are doing the "right thing," attending school and not joining gangs or using drugs, but that group is largely ignored. As a result, the "ugly" image many people have of South Central creates a division in terms of race, ethnicity, and class between ordinary South Central kids and USC students, who keep their distance from other residents.

Occasionally these two worlds meet, if ever so briefly, in classrooms of local schools when a group of USC students tutors kids, or when USC students jog past the kids on a run along Vermont Avenue, or at Ralphs's or Superior Supermarket's checkout counters—two of three supermarkets that serve a population of fifty thousand in what some consider to be one of the densest areas in Los Angeles and the United States.[4] These meetings do little to spark change in these groups, and so the inner-city kid world remains hidden, covered by a fear-provoking "ghetto thug" image.

The social distance between these two groups of South Central residents is made quite clear in my discussions with a class of twenty-one USC students who reside in student housing on or near the USC campus. I ask them if they are aware of the popular assumptions about kids like Kyle. Adam, who spent his childhood in a small Montana town, answers first: "Ghetto thug. I think most people see inner-city kids as poor, lazy, struggling, ghetto types who live in crime- and drug-ridden neighborhoods and who have bad parents." Several students nod in agreement. The rest remain silent. I do not suggest that all the college students hold these views. In Chapter 5, several college-student NAI tutors give us another perspective.

Nonetheless, the overriding image of inner-city kids' neighborhoods is far removed from Adam's description of the "comfortable" and "safe" neighborhoods of his childhood. Another student, Theresa, who rushes off to her family's home in Orange County every chance she gets, sums up her childhood years: "My middle school experiences were great because I went to a good school in a safe area, and my neighborhood had a similar dynamic. I was around good people with strong values." What impression did the USC students have of the railroad track photo and the area surrounding USC?

Theresa, who speaks up more than the rest, puts it this way: "Why would anyone want to live there? I'm terrified to walk off campus." All the students plan to leave the area after they graduate.

For middle-class students like Theresa, even if they do live down the street from these kids, the kids are made visible only when USC's campus police send out an e-mail alert that a USC student has been robbed by a hood-wearing troublemaker or a Black or Latino kid riding a bike. The USC students share the prevailing view of South Central. Therefore, the assumption that inner-city kids all end up in gangs, in prisons, or on drugs makes sense to them.

. . .

Three days a week, Kyle, Emma, and Maria rushed from their school classrooms to another class where they had to read another set of books and receive instructions from another group of teachers. I wondered what these kids, who were trying so hard to keep up with all of that work, had to say about the stigma of being an inner-city kid. In an attempt to examine this group of inner-city kids' lives both structurally and individually, the larger questions for me concern the following: How do these kids experience and react to the social problems associated with South Central? What do they think about their living conditions, family life, peer relations, and academic achievement in South Central, with its high concentration of social problems? How do they negotiate the challenges of living next door to the drug dealers, the gang members, and the friends who have dropped out of school? And why do they attend after-school programs when they could "hang out" with their peers?

The Neighborhood Academic Initiative Program

Some of the questions I raise in this book really began to take shape in 1997, when I had a chance to interview a group of kids in my position as a consultant for NAI.[5] The director at that time asked me to interview the kids to get their perspective on the program. I published the results of those interviews in an article titled "'It's Going Good': Inner-City Black and Latino Adolescents' Perceptions about Achieving an Education."[6] That study raised a number of questions about kids' perspectives of inner-city life that are explored in the current study, particularly those of kids who did not fit the stereotype of the ghetto thug. In that study, I suggested that adults often do not regard adolescents as having much interest in shaping the world they are going to inherit. Not so, I argued. These NAI kids were C students at risk for dropping out of school until their teachers took notice of their potential and recommended them for the tutorial program that would help them upgrade their math and English skills. The kids wanted to succeed academically and transcend their inner-city backgrounds.

The Neighborhood Academic Initiative, a seven-year college preparatory program, was established in 1989 at USC and was created to prepare low-income neighborhood students for admission to a college or university.[7] The Pre-College Enrichment Academy provides enhanced educational services to middle and high school students with the goal helping them acquire the academic skills they need to flourish in a college or university setting. The sixth-to-twelfth-grade program is composed of basic class material, tutoring, SAT tutoring, college counseling, supplementary material, and, in some cases, social worker support.

According to Robert Halpern, there is much consensus on what constitutes a good after-school program, though not necessarily a great one. Namely, a good after-school program needs an adequate number of staff to ensure individualized attention to children, an adequate level of staff literacy to help children with learning-support needs, adequate facilities and equipment to allow a measure of variety and choice in activities, and nutritious snacks for children. Important process attributes include warm and supportive staff; a flexible and relaxed schedule; a predictable environment; opportunities to explore ideas, feelings, and identities; avenues for self-expression; exposure to both one's own heritage and the larger culture; and time for unstructured play and fun.[8]

. . .

I began the research for this book in 2007 as a way to answer questions raised in the earlier study about kids' perceptions of life in South Central. I started my research by holding a focus group consisting of three minority USC students who could reflect on their early years living in the South Central community. This is an ideal group to interview because they have had a few years in which to gain a perspective on life in South Central. Yet they were still close enough in age to the kids in this study that they would be able to easily recall their kid years living in South Central.

I met two African Americans, twenty-year-olds Terry and Alicia, and Victor, a twenty-two-year-old Latino, at a café where they shared stories of their adolescent years over coffee and tea. I began by asking them questions such as the following: "What was it like for you growing up in South Central?" "What do you think of those experiences now that you are older and no longer living here?" They spoke for more than two hours, sometimes interrupting each other as they thought of more to say about living in South Central. Terry shared his view of growing up in South Central: "I think for myself, what I went through were experiences that most kids don't have. Like, I don't want to sound like the typical *Boyz n the Hood* drama story, but I actually had bullets whiz through my room when I was like four years old living in Watts." Terry's story about life in the inner city was confirmed by all of the kids who became part of the official study.

My next task was to seek out Black and Latino adolescents ages twelve to fifteen who lived in the South Central area, grew up in low-income working families, and would be considered average kids attending the local schools and not involved with drugs or gangs. I included a group of thirty-nine NAI kids in this study.

As a way to expand the pool to non-NAI kids who might have a different perspective of life in South Central, I contacted the Willard after-school program, another neighborhood program. I met and interviewed fifteen Willard kids ages fourteen to fifteen. This after-school program did not provide tutorial services or require parents to sign contracts or attend meetings. As with many after-school programs, Willard mainly served the kids as a safe place where they could receive homework assistance, play video games, and watch television. No other inner-city tutorial programs in the local area can match the NAI program's resources and commitment. The final group of kids who participated in this study consisted of fifty-four Black and Latino kids ages twelve to fifteen.

For this book, I conducted several focus groups and in-depth interviews with thirty-nine kids ages twelve to fifteen. Most had been in NAI for one to two years. All the kids came from families with annual incomes of $8,000 to $16,000. Half of them had brothers who were involved in gangs, and a few had sisters who were teenage mothers. The NAI kids' families must sign a contract stating that they will commit their families to the goals of the program by abiding by all the rules and attending a Saturday morning workshop offering new strategies related to issues concerning middle schoolers who, because they are in a demanding program, will face new challenges. If they stay in the program, graduate from high school, and earn passing SAT scores, they will be offered a financial aid package from USC, or they can apply to other university programs. According to NAI's Graduate Survey 1997–2011, over a sixteen-year period, an average of nearly forty NAI recipients per year graduated from the program; out of 635 graduates, 621 graduates went on to postsecondary education and 513 enrolled in four-year colleges (216 enrolled at USC).[9] Others were accepted in the UC and state systems as well as community colleges.

NAI also provides counseling services to help the kids and their families deal with changes in schoolwork habits and their relationships with parents and peers. According to the middle schoolers, NAI surrounded them with a combination of academic and nonacademic support services that profoundly affected three major areas of their lives: academic, social, and personal. These qualities instilled in the kids a feeling that they could work long and hard to achieve success, that they could be trustworthy, and that they were responsible to their teachers and peer members to develop the "habit of mind and character," qualities that Deborah Meier suggests are essential for overall educational success.[10] As twelve-year-old Cesar put it, "The program made our behavior into a more positive type of thing."

The Kids

None of the kids in that study conform to the views advanced by John Ogbu, who uses the concept of a "blocked opportunities framework" to explain why African American kids do not achieve academic success. Ogbu's study found that minority kids have a difficult time accomplishing much in life because they have developed a defiant attitude that actively rejects mainstream behaviors. That attitude has resulted in an "oppositional culture" effect, in which minority students who succeeded in school were considered to be "acting white."[11]

In Ogbu's study, African American high school students did poorly in school because they feared being accused of acting White by their peer group. Ogbu traces the roots of the problem of institutionalized racism within American society, which he contends led Blacks to define academic achievement as the prerogative of Whites and to invest themselves instead in alternative pursuits.[12]

The kids in this current study challenge Ogbu's "acting white" perspective. Many of them have made a commitment to complete all of their regular school demands as well as to do the extra schoolwork required by NAI both during the week and on Saturday mornings, which most middle schoolers would rather spend playing games or going to the movies with friends.

Thirteen-Year-Old Kyle

Late one afternoon, Kyle, one of the first NAI students to sign up to participate in this study, sits down to talk with me and to share photographs he has taken of his community, school, and family. He is a cheerful person who smiles widely when he talks about his school and his neighborhood. Kyle lives with his physically disabled mother and nine-year-old sister in a rented one-bedroom house on a street dotted with single-family homes and three-story apartment buildings in a South Central neighborhood, a mile past USC on Vermont and 32nd Place—a few blocks past a small grocery store plastered with "Don't Forget to Vote" signs in English and Spanish on its front door.

Kyle, a tall, lanky African American, flashing a bright smile, disagrees with the "ghetto thug" assessment by "outsiders"—a term used to describe people who live outside South Central. Like most other Latino and Black kids I talk to, Kyle thinks most people have a negative view of him. It is hard for someone like Kyle, who is growing up in an impoverished inner-city neighborhood, to understand that his world, through the NAI program, is linked to privileged college students who are able and willing to share valuable social resources. Kyle and the other fifty-three kids say that getting an education is uppermost in their minds. They also say that spending time after school in a positive environment where they can "hang out" with other students like themselves and not on the streets is also important.

Kyle is proud of his home—never mind that the photographs he spreads around the table show a one-story house in desperate need of paint and repair (see Figure 1.2): "I like my house and block. I know everybody. That's good about where I live—it's not wealthy, but I can play basketball and ride my bike about because there are no gangs near my house." His response to the general perception of inner-city kids?

> Most people see kids like me as inner-city gangbangers. I don't wanna be a gangbanger. That judges me and how I act. I don't do that stuff. It makes the community look bad. Um, like some people say that, like where you live, says how smart you are or how dumb. But I don't think that's possible because I live in, like, a pretty bad neighborhood, but I'm still, like, a bright kid. I take all AP classes.

Kyle has plans. They differ from those of the college students who plan to study history, or "major in soc," or become a social worker. Kyle, a handsome

Figure 1.2

ninth grader, plans to play professional basketball or become a mechanic. When pressed about his future plans, he says he is good at basketball and "wants to make lots of money like Kobe Bryant." If that plan does not work, "I'm good with my hands, so I can become a mechanic." He says he is "very good in math," but he has no plans to use that skill in the future.

There are times, Kyle admits, when he does not feel safe on some of the streets in his neighborhood, like the time Emmi, a petite fourteen-year-old who sits next to him and faintly smiles whenever he speaks, warned him as he walked her home: "The Crips and Bloods live down the block from me and across the street from each other. So I don't walk down that street." Although Kyle likes his neighborhood, Emma admits being afraid to play outside and says that if she rides her bike outside, she stays alert to drive-by shootings by the violent street gangs that often patrol her street.[13]

Kyle also fears the pit bull owned by the next-door neighbors. According to Kyle, one day the dog jumped over a fence that separates his house from that of the neighbors. "The dog rushed at my mother. She was scared. But we got her into the house right away and the dog didn't get her. There are a lot of those dogs in this neighborhood. If he comes after my mother again, I will beat him and kill him."[14] Ironically, these kids, who are commonly assumed to be "ghetto thugs" but are involved in a tutorial program that promises a way out of poverty, live in fear of the same South Central neighborhoods that scare the college students.

Studying Inner-City Youth

Sociologists have examined many aspects of inner-city life, including its effects on kids who have had to deal with drugs, gangs, unemployment, and low academic achievement.[15] These classic ethnographies have revealed a world of street youth in which unemployment is rampant, teenage pregnancy is common, and social and educational achievement is viewed as "acting White." These studies show that institutional racism is a major factor in this condition and the behavior exhibited by inner-city kids. They also demonstrate that one's race, ethnicity, and social class have a massive influence on where one lives, the kind of school one will attend, and where on the social hierarchy one will end up. Although a few studies include kids who are successful in school, most focus on the lives of kids who are flunking in school or have quit altogether.

These thought-provoking studies are the impassioned inside story of how America looks from the bottom and have added great insight into the lives of inner-city kids. Although as Jay MacLeod[16] and Mitchell Duneier[17] point out, social mobility is possible, the overall structure of class, race, and ethnic relations remains unchanged. Duneier suggests in his book *Sidewalk* that "through a careful involvement in people's lives, we can get a fix on how their world works and how they see it. But the details can be misleading if they distract us from the forces that are less visible to the people we observe but which influence and sustain the behaviors."[18]

Still, I think there is more to be said about these kids. Perhaps it was my own experience as an inner-city kid growing up in Harlem, considered to be the first Black ghetto, or perhaps it was my previous study of a group of South Central kids, that led me to believe that we do not know enough about these kids.

Where One Lives Matters

"Negative images of inner-city kids are not new. If you grow up in the South Bronx or South Central Los Angeles or Pittsburgh or Philadelphia, you quickly come to understand that you have been set apart and that there's no will in this society to bring them back into the mainstream."[19] I grew up in Harlem, an area considered the first Black urban ghetto. During the 1940s,

Harlem was the place to go nightclubbing for rich White sophisticates. By the time I reached my teen years, the glamour of the Harlem Renaissance had long been replaced with the blight of urban ugliness. During the 1960s, Harlem began to decline socially, economically, and culturally. Heroin sold by such notorious drug lords as Bumpy Johnson and Frank Lucas found its way into the community.[20] Prosperous and middle-class Blacks moved out of Harlem to other areas of New York City and its suburbs, leaving poor and working-class Blacks to live in rented, crowded tenements. Mostly, Eastern European immigrants owned the mom-and-pop businesses in the community.

Harlem may have been a ghetto to some, but to many of its residents, it was home. The children there also found fun things to do. They jumped rope and played Simon Says, dodgeball, and basketball while cars whizzed around the players. "Outsiders" were often quite disdainful of inner-city residents, whom they considered low-class, criminal types who were too dumb or lazy to do anything but live in poverty. I remember the murmured comments from outsiders: "Those kids," they often said, applying a culture-of-poverty rationale, "who are playing street games today will be out robbing you or taking drugs tomorrow."

"Those kids" may have been handed a bad rap by outsiders, but they did have an advantage over South Central kids. While Harlem might have seemed like a segregated community to many analysts, it was not as isolated from the larger city life as South Central, a car-dependent community. Every week, the renowned Apollo Theater played to sold-out racially mixed audiences to hear legendary artists such as Miles Davis, James Brown, and Aretha Franklin or to dine at Ethel's Southern Quarters, a popular soul food restaurant. In warm weather, parents sat on front stoops to escape their hot apartments, watch the children play, and gossip with friends.

In recent years, Harlem has changed. Now you can take a tour bus to visit former president Bill Clinton's suite of offices on 125th Street, where you will also get caught up in a crowd of Black, Latino, and White kids and their families shopping at the Gap or buying hamburgers from McDonald's. It would be quite easy to conclude that if poor and scary Harlem can change, other inner cities will follow suit. Actually, Harlem's physical layout—being located close to midtown Manhattan—means that most public transportation (buses and subways) has to go through Harlem. Many people use the public transportation system, since parking is limited and parking lots cost anywhere from $10 to $25 an hour. Anyone using public transportation to go to the Bronx or downtown Manhattan has to pass 125th Street. It is also easy for Harlem residents to use public transportation to go into midtown or downtown Manhattan. In fact, so many people take the train to and from Harlem that the directions were immortalized when composer and orchestra leader Duke Ellington gave directions to his collaborator, Billy Strayhorn, who promptly wrote them down as lyrics for "Take the A Train," a song that became the signature of the Ellington orchestra.[21]

In other words, it is much more difficult to avoid or hide the Harlem ghetto than it is to hide the South Central ghetto. The only people to see musical artists in South Central tend to be other inner-city residents. If they want to hear Carlos Santana, Los Lonely Boys, or Jay-Z, they have to see them at Staples Center or some other large entertainment arena, not in South Central. Manhattan has more geographically compressed urban areas like Harlem; Los Angeles's sprawl and dependence on cars mean that the city is likely to be far removed from the world of inner-city kids. One has to have some reason to travel into South Central. Still, Harlem's history of drastic socioeconomic changes—of moving from wealth to poverty—is similar to that of South Central.

The earlier NAI study raised questions about the experiences of South Central kids who live in an area so synonymous with urban decay and street crime that the city council tried to change its image by changing its name.[22] While this book also examines inner-city life from the perspective of those at the bottom of the class, race, and ethnic hierarchy, it goes further than previous studies. In this study, a group of South Central inner-city kids examined their own lives both structurally and individually by exposing their living conditions, family life, peer relations, and academic achievement in South Central. In their view, we have failed to grasp the problems they confront on a daily basis or to understand the extent to which they feel shunned, hidden, forgotten—by a society that has reduced them to a pejorative, to being less than human, therefore reinforcing their feelings of being socially isolated from the larger society.

My focus on kids who have the desire to succeed and who receive a great deal of social support, particularly from USC's tutorial program, situates this group far away from the gang-involved, violent, or abused kids who dominate the literature on inner-city kids. Cesar, Kyle, Wynette, and the others present an alternative to the limited view of these kids as being losers. Their stories challenge the popular view that inner-city kids are primarily dysfunctional, worthless, ghetto gangsters. They present a unique take on their world, one that gives deep insight into what life is like for many inner-city kids. Kyle and others in this study face an ongoing struggle with feelings of ambivalence about their lives, as first expressed in their analysis of the railroad track picture.

Poverty of Relationships

Structural issues are essential in this story. But also important to consider is the other story that the kids seem intent on telling us, which has to do with their sense of worth, or, in this case, their sense of worthlessness that comes with the tag "ghetto thug" (as described by Adam, the USC student quoted previously).

Along with the ghetto thug myth, I try to dismantle a number of other myths about inner-city kids, the principal one being that all inner-city kids' behaviors are encouraged by parents with bad jobs and bad attitudes who act as role models for their kids' bad behaviors. I argue that these kids need a better-funded community. But they also need stronger relationships with members of their community. They need parents like most in this book, who go to great lengths to protect their kids. The kids in this book say that they need teachers and an educational system in general that understand adolescence as a special time of life—one in which they begin to think about that all-important question "Who am I?"[23]

The questions I raised in another study are also relevant here: What happens to interpersonal relationships when adolescents and their families are trying to leap a fence and instead find themselves still stuck in stereotypes whose main function is to keep them rooted in their assumed place in society? What kind of strategies do they develop to compensate for the loss of societal support? I suggest that, in general, these kids suffer from a general sense of the loss of connections (1) with their community and (2) with the larger society. The sociology of emotions is key to understanding how significant relationships are to our emotional well-being. Sociologist Norman Denzin argues in his book *On Understanding Emotion* that it is important to examine the personal, psychological, social, and cultural aspects of human emotion—how people experience joy and pain, love and hate, anger and despair, friendship and alienation—in order to understand human experience and social interactions.[24]

I propose that we tend to give little thought to the impact of relational poverty on the lives of kids who do not have society's support. In my book on teenage mothers, I used the term *poverty of relationships*. That term also applies to these kids' sense of alienation and isolation. The poverty-of-relationships theory suggests that institutional oppression does exist and is played out in a relational framework in which these kids develop strategies to form and sustain relationships with their peer groups and others who lend them support during a time of life when positive relationships are key to their sense of self. In other words, it is important to emphasize how the kids grapple with their emotional feelings about their status in society. They develop their own strategies to compensate for their sense of not having a place in the larger social world. Studies show that kids become involved in gangs and teenage girls have babies as ways to make up for the social support missing in their lives. Understanding this concept of poverty of relationships and how it applies to the kids links it to Denzin's sociology-of-emotions theory in this way: These kids may be seen as "striver" kids, as NAI director Kim Thomas-Barrios, suggests. But even as strivers, they feel so isolated and alienated that the only safe havens they think they have are these after-school programs. Being an inner-city "striver" does not pay off, at least psychologically as one would hope, since most people still perceive them to be ghetto thugs.

■   ■   ■

"We Live in the Shadow" offers new insights and strategies to address the social and emotional problems of inner-city kids and makes explicit the complexities specific to academically oriented inner-city minority kids. Throughout this book, the kids protest the idea that they are hood-wearing "ghetto thugs" who live on the wrong side of the railroad track; these teenagers are working hard to become productive citizens. Despite that effort, everything they encounter seems to be working against them: the school system, the perspective that they are losers, and the disorderliness of their neighborhood. All seem designed to make them fail. These teens, instead, actively pursue another view of themselves to counter the negative one.

This book is organized around the major idea that the inner-city kids in this study have developed a complex way of seeing society. They see society as making them feel isolated from and alienated by the larger mainstream society. They bring a strong sense to this book that their lives and the streets they live on are disorderly and sources of distasteful and worrisome encounters that they must endure because they live in South Central. As one person put it, these kids are "floating just above water." In the end, the kids will say, in the words of comedian Chris Rock, "Don't hate the player; hate the game."

2 |

The Photovoice Methodology

For this project, I draw on Jay MacLeod's idea that the stories of kids from poor neighborhoods "are less often told and much less heard." But we must listen, he argues, because they "provide a poignant account of what the social structure looks like from the bottom."[1] The idea of thinking about life from the perspectives of kids became quite clear to me as a way of conducting research on inner-city kids when I saw the 2004 documentary *Born into Brothels: Calcutta's Red Light Kids*,[2] about the inspiring nonprofit foundation Kids with Cameras, which teaches photography skills to children in marginalized communities. In 1998, photographer Zana Briski started photographing prostitutes in the red-light district of Calcutta. The filmmakers inspired a special group of children of the prostitutes to photograph the district's more reluctant subjects. As the kids excel in their newfound art, the filmmakers struggle to help them have a chance for a better life away from the miserable poverty that threatens to crush their dreams.

I remember walking out of the theater thinking about how much I had learned about the kids' perspectives from their photos. I also saw how much the kids enjoyed taking the photos and being in charge of presenting their lives. I wanted to know more about this methodology.

Photovoice was developed by Caroline Wang and Mary Ann Burris, program officer for women's health at the Ford Foundation.[3] In 1992, Wang and Burris created Photo Novella, now known as photovoice, as a way to enable rural women of Yunnan Province, China, to influence the policies and programs that affected them. They report being strongly influenced by the efforts of Nina Wallerstein and Edward Bernstein, who adapted the ideas of Paulo Freire's *Pedagogy of the Oppressed* to health promotion and education. It has since been used among homeless adults in Ann Arbor, Michigan, and among community health workers and teachers in rural South Africa. Wang and Burris suggest that this methodology is particularly useful in allowing marginalized people to give weight to how they conceptualize their circumstances and their hopes for the future.[4]

According to the literature, the photovoice methodology enables people in need to document their lives as only they can really know them.[5] According to PhotoVoice, an organization that designs programs using the photovoice methodology, its mission is to build skills within disadvantaged and marginalized communities "using innovative participatory photography and digital storytelling methods so that they have the opportunity to represent themselves and create tools for advocacy and communications to achieve positive social change."[6] As noted in another article, nongovernmental organizations (NGOs) and community organizations have used photovoice, a method the authors described as participatory photography, digital storytelling, and self-advocacy projects for socially excluded groups.[7] This pioneering approach brings together the arts, media, development, and social change agendas to work with hard-to-reach groups on projects that give voice, build skills, provide platforms for advocacy, and work toward sustainable change.

Why Photography Is Useful to Sociology

As *Born into Brothels* demonstrates, photography is a highly flexible tool that crosses cultural and linguistic barriers and can be adapted to all abilities. Its power lies in its dual role as an art form and a means to record facts. It provides an accessible way to define realities, communicate perspectives, and raise awareness of important social and global issues. Its low cost and ease of dissemination encourage sharing and increase the potential to generate dialogue and discussion. In this study, the meaningfulness of this methodology is made clear in the ways in which the social worlds of these inner-city kids both converged with and diverged from those of the USC students who also live, albeit only until graduation, in the inner city.

Photovoice allows projects like this one to channel the unique subjectivity of the participants into a direct and powerful form of human communication. In truth, photovoice projects enlarge the lives of their participants and ours, too. Through witnessing the daily challenges of select groups as they see them, we get closer to truly understanding their lives and needs and are perhaps moved ourselves to help bring about change. In other words, the kids in this study take on the role of participant observer (although when we move deeper into the study, I become what I would call a partial observer of some aspects of the community).

Using Photovoice for This Study

I began this study with the expectation that photovoice methodology would give voice to the kids' perspectives on their experiences in an inner-city community, and throughout the study, it proves to be an invaluable tool.[8] The photovoice method also allowed me to initiate a more youth-centered dialogue that I think reveals personal and community issues through the kids' own cognitions and perceptions of their lives.[9] This method, also called the photo-essay, provides an once-in-a-lifetime opportunity for the kids to document and express their experiences through personally meaningful imagery. Unlike other studies, the kids are in charge of representing themselves and their community within their own frame of reference, allowing me to produce a study that goes further than other studies. Using the photovoice method also allows me to develop what Clifford Geertz calls a layered and deep interpretation of a social issue.[10]

In this study, I identify a number of questions I want the kids to respond to in order to understand how their academic and personal objectives can change with collaborative efforts, for instance with programs such as NAI and the Willard after-school program. But since kids are known for limiting their answers to adult inquiry to "yes" or "no," I thought the photovoice method would be quite useful. According to psychologist and art therapist Christine Cordone, these photos allow children to express their internal world through personally meaningful imagery.[11] Cordone, who has used this method in her therapy practice, suggests that it is important to let children express themselves without any influence from an adult. In this way, photographs help us understand the children's perceptions and feelings about what is happening to them and allow us to explore alternative solutions that we may not think of, without their responses to that material.

Estela Beale, a child and adult psychiatrist, also uses this method in her practice and argues that children can express what is uppermost in their minds more genuinely and spontaneously. "This helps to contain some of

the anxieties they are experiencing, which can lead to reframing or express-
ing things in a different way."[12]

The rich and often poignant stories derived from the photovoice method
provide us with a way to produce an analysis of the lives of these inner-city
kids that deepens and enhances current theory by making explicit the complexities surrounding their lives. Wang, Burris, and Beale also show that
photovoice has three main goals that I found useful for this study:

1. To enable people to record and reflect their community's
   strengths and concerns
2. To promote critical dialogue and knowledge about personal and
   community issues through large- and small-group discussions of
   photographs
3. To reach policy makers

The photovoice method was extremely useful to this study for five rea-
sons: (1) Giving the kids cameras to take pictures of their experiences enabled them to record and reflect their own likes and dislikes and concerns.
(2) This method helped me initiate a youth-centered dialogue in the interviews with kids and helped me discover personal and community issues
through the cognitive development and perceptions of the kids. (3) This
method also provided a special opportunity for the kids to document and
express their experiences through personally meaningful imagery. (4) The
photovoice method allowed the kids to take charge of representing themselves and their community within their own frame of reference. (5) Most
important, the photos allowed the kids to drive the narrative of their lives,
thereby introducing us to areas of their lives to which we might not otherwise have had access. The kids took 531 photographs, of which 53 were used
as representative.[13]

The photovoice method also allows the sociologist to use what C. Wright
Mills calls the sociological imagination.[14] As Mills saw it, having sociological
imagination is critical for individual people and societies at large to understand. It is important that people can relate the situations in which they live
their daily lives to the local, national, and global societal issues that affect
them. Without the ability to make these relations, people cannot see societal
issues that affect them and cannot determine whether these issues require
change to better their everyday lives. The kids in this study certainly knew
how to use their sociological imagination in telling stories of their inner-city
experiences.

The Interviewing Process

All of the kids were required to take part in two interviews. I met with the directors of NAI and Willard and the kids separately and for an hour each. All of the students were engaging with the counselors and peers involved with the after-school programs, which meant that in their eyes I was someone who allowed them to talk about experiences. They would participate because the counselors and others in their support system suggested that they would enjoy the experience.

At the first meeting I discussed the procedure for using the photovoice method. I handed each kid a five-dollar disposable camera and made only a few suggestions, such as "Take pictures of anything you want to show me about your experiences." I instructed the kids to photograph anything that characterized their community. The photo assignment asked them to "take pictures of your neighborhood, your favorite places, your least favorite places." Another photo assignment asked them to "take pictures of your friends, schools, teachers, and homework assignments you like, don't like" and "anything else you want to talk about."

I informed them of the human subjects protocol: that they should not take photos of anything or anyone that posed a threat to them—for example, people who were involved in gangs. I advised the kids to ask for permission before taking photos of anyone. If for any reason they did not like the photos they took or lost the camera, they were not to worry but should ask for another one. The kids were given a one-week deadline for turning in their cameras to me or one of the associates.

The second interview took place after I had the photos printed. At the beginning of the second interview, I handed back the pictures and asked straightforward questions such as "Why did you take that picture?" "What did you want me to know about you based on this picture?" At the end of the photo sessions, the kids selected the photos they wanted bound and returned to them as mementos. My research associate, Emir Loy, created for them photo CDs and a certificate acknowledging their assistance in the study. We gave these items out at a large meeting that was also attended by a few parents. We also showed them some of the photos. Judging from one of the photos twelve-year-old Cesar shared with his group, he really liked taking photos with his camera (see Figure 2.1). Everyone laughed and clapped at his comment on the photo.

Often the kids would use the photos as a way to set up the story line—a way to ease into talking about their experiences. The pictures took us onto

Figure 2.1

the streets where they lived, into their classrooms and bedrooms, and onto the USC campus. The photographs taken by the kids gave a view of their lives that we frequently miss in our attempt to apply our own perceptions of their lives, as did the USC students.

In this study, the photovoice method enabled the fifty-four kids to think critically about their community and to discuss their everyday life in ways that add to my understanding of the social and political forces that influence their lives. Throughout this book, we see kids using their photos to contest the subjugation, rules, regulations, and authority that have attempted to restrict and restrain them. These photos also generate strong emotional reactions and debates. For example, recall the kids' comments about Kyle's railroad track photos and the twenty-one USC students' response to that same photo. In later chapters, fifteen parents as well as other adults respond to these photographs.

These kids' comments about their lives are both surprising and thought-provoking. The biggest surprise to me is that they took this project to heart. I did not expect them to present me with a sociological analysis but rather to take the easy way out by shooting pictures of their friends, lose their cameras, or just forget to take pictures. But none of those problems occurred. I came away from this project with the sense that these kids were not only brilliant in their interpretations of the structures that governed their lives but brilliant in knowing how to convey that information in the photos for this research. They seemed intent on using their photos to change the false narrative, to present an alternative view of them. Some used their photos of car wreckage, for example, as metaphors for their potentially ruinous inner-city lives. I had to rethink my assumptions that as an adult who once lived in an inner-city community, I would have a better understanding of their lives than would these kids.

I also would venture to say that this kind of qualitative research catches the nuance of kids' experiences that can lead to the development of real questions for quantitative work. By using questions developed during qualitative research, we can get people to talk informally about their lives in a way that raises questions useful for larger community studies on, for example, South Central. This book's findings tell us that until we hear people actually talk about their concerns, we do not know the right kinds of questions to ask.

The Interactionist Approach

The approach of using both the kids' photographs and interviews allows us to see that everyday interactions involve self-concept and identity, which are formed by their interactions with teachers, parents, and peers. Sociology teaches us that it is in interactions with others, through the socialization process, that children develop an understanding of moral values, how families behave, and policies and laws. In one way or another, all of these themes have an impact on kids' interactions with others and how they see themselves.

The interactionist approach allows me to investigate how the kids interpret their lives as well as how they see other people's actions and to see whether the consequences of their interpretation will be played out in the larger social group. As W. I. Thomas says, "It is not important whether or not the interpretation is correct—if [people] define situations as real, they are real in their consequence."[15] According to symbolic interactionism, society and its organizations are basically the outcome of past symbolic interactions and negotiators. It is important to note, however, that if it is true, as symbolic interactionists argue, that social change does not happen when external factors change, then it happens when people assign new meanings to situations and therefore act accordingly.

In the case of the kids in this study, the main objective of this book is to show that the larger society has to reach a new understanding of and assign new meaning to the experiences of inner-city kids. The second objective is to show that these kids have taken on that task themselves by using the photos as a way to tell their stories and thereby give new meaning to their lives as inner-city minority kids. As the kids and other participants tell their stories, the third objective is to use the photos and comments to show how social inequality can be reproduced on a daily basis in the kids' lives. While the kids are in charge of their perceptions, my role is to connect the dots, so to speak, by linking their perceptions in such a way as to make as clear as possible the multiple realities of these kids.

The interviews and photographs reveal inner-city life from the perspectives of a group of fifty-four kids, most of whom are trying to turn around their lives in one way or another; how they understand those experiences; and how they explain those experiences. Another set of issues that this study explores involves the extent to which living in South Central affects their sense of self-worth, in terms of how they see themselves.

With this idea in mind, this study moves away from social theories that explain how the world *is*, rather than how the participants *see* it. For example, the kids tell us, through photos, about their lives within their neighborhood and why it is important to the sense of their world. My other role is to check their interpretations with theories and other interviews and data.

In an analysis that includes comments about photos and interviews, the kids tell us what it means to face a double disadvantage that comes from belonging to a minority group and being trapped in economically devastated neighborhoods where few kids graduate from high school. If they find work at all, it will likely be at low-wage jobs. Through the photos and interviews we not only catch the kids' ambivalence about their lives but also get an up-close and personal look at what it means to live in an isolated community. Their interpretation at this moment is captured in their photographs and interviews. The kids may change their perspective at a later date, although I doubt it, since Terry, Alicia, and Victor, the three inner-city USC students mentioned previously, do not. "It is a pissy experience, living in the ghetto," Terry says.

What surprised me most is that the kids seemed determined to carry out the study instructions, although the NAI director did have to tell two kids that they needed to participate in the study. Initially, I expected that most of their photos would not be printable or would mainly be of their friends. Instead, they eagerly participated and willingly gave their views on anything, including their feelings about the presidential candidates. Another surprise had to do with learning that my own sense of what these photos said was way off base.

In this study, the kids develop powerful themes about social class, race, and ethnic inequality and to some extent gender inequality, power, and dominance. They also tell us in their own way about the ways in which trust and responsibility should work but in their view do not. In fact, their openness shows them to be quite intent on lending their voices to sociological and political discourse about kids' inner-city life.

II

History and Transformation
of South Central

3 |

"Don't Be a Menace to South Central while Drinking Your Juice in the Hood"

The History and Transformation of the Inner City

L os Angeles, like other large urban centers (New York City, for example), is a big place with lots of people. Unlike New York City, Los Angeles has long been noted for its sprawling major commercial, financial, and cultural institutions, which are geographically dispersed rather than being concentrated in a single downtown or central area.[1] It also makes sense, then, for Los Angeles to be known as a city of car-dependent communities. The term *urban sprawl* generally has negative connotations because of the health, environmental, and cultural issues associated with the phrase. Residents of sprawling neighborhoods tend to emit more pollution per person and suffer more traffic fatalities.[2]

Nicknamed the City of Angels, the Entertainment Capital of the World, and La-La Land, Los Angeles is considered a leading world center of business, international trade, entertainment, culture, media, fashion, science, sports, technology, and education, and it has been ranked the third-richest city and fifth most powerful and influential city in the world. The city is home to renowned institutions covering a broad range of professional and cultural fields and is one of the most substantial economic engines within the United States, making it the third-largest economic center in the world, after the Greater Tokyo and New York metropolitan areas. The Entertainment Capital of the World, as the home base of Hollywood, is also known to lead the world in the creation of motion pictures, television productions, stage productions, video games, and recorded music. The importance of the entertainment business to the city has led many celebrities to call Los Angeles and its surrounding suburbs home. Additionally, Los Angeles hosted the Summer Olympics in 1932 and 1984. It has been recognized as the most diverse of the nation's largest cities.[3]

Of course, like most large cities, Los Angeles has a side that only minorities and the poor and working class see—a repository of ethnic groups, low-skill jobs, a large service and informal economy, and a host of other low-paying occupations that residents tend to see as being related to racism and nativity status.

According to the author of the report "Concentrated Poverty Neighborhoods in Los Angeles," Los Angeles is one of only two major metropolitan areas in which concentrated poverty became more prevalent between 1990 and 2000.[4] The author "found that neighborhoods with concentrated poverty are clustered in a corridor extending from downtown-adjacent neighborhoods to South Los Angeles."[5] The findings point to four serious social problems in these areas: (1) 8 percent of the tracts in the city have concentrated levels of poverty, and these tracts are home to 15 percent of all the city's households in poverty; (2) residents of concentrated poverty neighborhoods are disproportionately Latino and Black; (3) residents in these areas are less likely to be employed and more likely to be out of the labor force; and (4) these residents tend to experience widespread impacts of indicators of social well-being and are 63 percent more adversely affected than the city as a whole by housing insecurity, immobility, educational attainments, school performance, young adults at risk, maternal health outcomes, and public safety.[6] These problems serve as a backdrop for the images produced by the South Central kids in this study.

History of South Central: "The Gang Capital of America"

South Los Angeles, often abbreviated as South L.A., is the official name for a large geographic and cultural area southwest and southeast of downtown Los Angeles, California. The area, formerly called South Central Los Angeles and still widely known as "South Central," has become almost synonymous with urban decay and street crime.[7] While attempts have been made to gentrify areas such as Baldwin Hills, Crenshaw, and Leimert Park, there are neighborhoods where if kids like Kyle or Cesar play street games, they can easily become victims of drive-by shootings.

Negative images tend to blur some of the other interesting factors about South Central. For example, South L.A. contains some of the oldest neighborhoods in Los Angeles, featuring many spectacular examples of Victorian and Craftsman architecture in West Adams. This area is also the site of USC, founded in 1880, as well as the Doheny Campus of Mount St. Mary's College, founded in 1920. South Central also hosted the 1932 and 1984 Olympic Games, which took place near the USC campus at neighboring Exposition Park.[8]

Until the 1920s, when the development of the Wilshire Boulevard corridor drew L.A. businesses to the west of downtown, West Adams was considered one of the most desirable areas of the city. Wealthy businessmen built stately mansions in West Adams and Jefferson Park, while the White working class established itself in Crenshaw and Hyde Park. Well-known figures such as L.A. County Supervisor Yvonne Brathwaite Burke, artist Jackson Pollock, California state senator Mark Ridley-Thomas, and actor Paul Winfield attended schools in South Central.[9] These and other affluent Blacks purchased property and gradually moved into West Adams and Jefferson Park as the decades passed. At the same time, South Central was one of the first jazz scenes in the western United States, with trombonist Kid Ory a prominent resident.[10]

Under racially restrictive covenants, Blacks were allowed to own property only within the Main-Saloon-Alameda-Washington box and in Watts, as well as in small enclaves elsewhere in the city. The working- and middle-class Blacks who poured into Los Angeles during the Great Depression and for jobs during World War II found themselves penned into what is becoming a severely overcrowded neighborhood. During the war, Blacks faced such dire housing shortages that the Housing Authority of the City of Los Angeles built the virtually all-Black Pueblo Del Rio project, in opposition to its previous stated policy of integrating all city housing projects.[11]

When the Supreme Court banned the legal enforcement of race-oriented restrictive covenants in 1948 (*Shelley v. Kraemer*), Blacks begin to move into areas outside the increasingly overcrowded Main-Saloon-Alameda-Washington settlement area.[12] In the early 1950s, southern Los Angeles became the site of significant racial violence, with Whites bombing, shooting into, and burning crosses on the lawns of homes of Black families. Escalating behavior that began in the 1920s, White gangs, one with the name White Spook Hunters, enforced boundary transgressions; when backup was needed, it was supplied by the Los Angeles Police Department (LAPD).[13]

White gangs routinely accosted Blacks who traveled through White areas. The Black mutual-protection clubs that formed in response to these assaults evolved into the region's most formidable street gangs, the Crips and the Bloods.[14] According to the LAPD, the city is home to 45,000 gang members, organized into 450 gangs.[15] Among them are the Crips and Bloods, which are both African American street gangs that originated in South Central Los Angeles. Several Latino street gangs, such as the Sureños, a Mexican American street gang, and the Mara Salvatrucha, which has mainly members of Central American origin, also originated in Los Angeles, as did the 18th Street gang, which has a predominately Latino membership but is multiethnic. This has led to the city being referred to as the "Gang Capital of America."[16]

New York's sporadic cycles of gang violence have never paralleled the deadly carnage experienced in Los Angeles. In *Street Wars*, Tom Hayden's insightful study of gangs, Hayden writes that some ten thousand of Los Angeles's young people have been killed in gang conflicts over the past two decades.[17] The LAPD reported 11,402 gang-related crimes in 2005. That same year, the New York Police Department (NYPD) reported just 520. Federal Bureau of Investigation (FBI) crime reports indicate that New York's homicide rate that year was about half that of Los Angeles, while the rate of reported gang crime in Los Angeles was forty-nine times the rate reported in New York City.[18]

The explosive growth of suburbs just outside Los Angeles, most of which barred Blacks by a variety of methods, provided the opportunity for Whites in neighborhoods bordering Black districts to leave in droves. The spread of Blacks throughout the area was achieved in large part through "blockbusting," a technique whereby real estate speculators buy a home on an all-White street, sell or rent it to a Black family, and then buy up the remaining homes from Whites at cut-rate prices and sell them at a hefty profit to housing-hungry Blacks. This process accelerated after the Watts Riot of 1965.

The Watts Riots were a civil disturbance in the Watts neighborhood from August 11 to August 17, 1965, that began when racial tensions reached a breaking point after two White policemen scuffled with a Black motorist suspected of drunken driving. The riots resulted in the abandonment of southern Los Angeles by White residents and merchants as well as middle-class Blacks. Roberta James, a parent of one of the kids in the study, mentioned the riots in her comments about life in South Central. "Everything burned down in South Central, except USC," she said with a laugh.

By the 1970s, the decline of the area's manufacturing base resulted in the loss of skilled middle-class union workers. African Americans earning relatively high wages were replaced by newly arrived Central American immigrants. One journalist writes about that time, "Money ran short. Rats moved in. In the 1970s, even the playground got paved over."[19] South Central had undergone a number of changes. Though it had once been an area of middle-to-lower-income Black families, its manufacturing base declined in the 1970s, resulting in the loss of jobs that had allowed skilled union workers to have a middle-class life. At the same time, widespread unemployment, poverty, and street crime resulted in South Central street gangs such as the Crips and the Bloods becoming a powerful force backed by money from drugs, especially the crack cocaine trade, in the 1980s.[20]

The demography of South Los Angeles has been changing since the late 1980s, as immigrants from Mexico and Central America have arrived in numbers to buy or rent apartments and homes, some of which have been vacated by African American renters. Before the 1990s, South Central's largest population consisted mainly of African Americans (80 percent in 1980).[21]

To add to the growing economic problems, South Central had become a haven for gangs and dealers selling crack and other drugs. In 1991, the rapper Ice Cube recorded "How to Survive in South Central," essentially an instruction manual for working-class Blacks in a neighborhood he calls "the concrete Vietnam." The song, along with other rap lyrics from the soundtrack of John Singleton's film *Boyz n the Hood*, bolstered the public image of South Central as a gangster-controlled zone of Black violence and urban struggle.[22]

By the time of the 1992 Los Angeles riots, which began in South Central and spread throughout the city, South Central had become a byword for urban decline. This image was strengthened by skewed media coverage of the 1992 riots that made the area synonymous with crime, gangs, unemployment, blight, riots, and racial tensions. The Los Angeles riots of 1992 started on April 29, after a jury trial resulted in the acquittal of four LAPD officers accused in the videotaped beating of motorist Rodney King following a high-speed police pursuit. Thousands of people throughout the Los Angeles metropolitan area rioted for six days following the announcement of the verdict. Fifty-three people were killed during the riots, and more than two thousand people were injured.

South Central's bad reputation is also played up in movies such as *Colors*, *South Central*, *Menace II Society*, and *Friday*. Adding to that bad image was the rap group N.W.A's album *Straight Outta Compton*, promoting South Central's gang life.

"This Is South Central"

"There are so many crackheads and like homeless people here," fourteen-year-old Maria says in response to my question "Are these pictures of your neighborhood?" When I began interviewing the group of fifty-four kids during 2007–2008, the downtown L.A. service sector, long dominated by unionized African Americans earning relatively high wages, had replaced most Black workers with newly arrived Central American immigrants. The dramatic growth in joblessness and economic downturns tied to national recession had in turn created economic crises in South Central.

On December 28, 2012, the *Los Angeles Times* reported that despite the general decline of crime throughout the city, "the figures also underscored the stark geographic disparities of where crime occurs in Los Angeles. In the wealthy Westside neighborhoods patrolled by the LAPD's West L.A. Division, there were 276 violent crimes, while the neighborhoods of South L.A. experienced about five times that number."[23]

The economic restructuring also set in motion a process that Loic Wacquant and William J. Wilson suggest is an extreme concentration of poor minorities in inner cities with high unemployment, deteriorated housing, and declining graduation rates.[24] This condition, known as hyperghettoization, creates an even bigger income inequality both locally and across the nation, for example, in cities such as Detroit and Philadelphia. Nonetheless, the authors note, these inner-city communities are protected during the restructuring phase by male adults, "old heads." Elijah Anderson uses the term *old head* to describe "a man of stable means who believed in hard work, family life and the church."[25] Anderson continues, "He was an aggressive agent of the wider society whose acknowledged role was to teach, support, encourage and in effect watch over a Philadelphia inner-city neighborhood and its children and who frowns on signs of criminal activity."[26]

In Anderson's book *Codes of the Street*, Mr. Moses serves as an example of an old head—"the epitome of the decent daddy, playing the role not only in his own household but also in the neighborhood, providing especially strong support to the local children and, in doing so, playing the part of the old head."[27] Today, however, in inner-city neighborhoods, the old heads have been replaced by the streets, having lost out to a high-tech labor market for which they do not qualify or to low-wage labor jobs. You can certainly see those signs in South Central neighborhoods, where supportive role models are almost nonexistent.

■ ■ ■

Several times a week, I drive down the streets of South Central. As I drive down a few of the streets near the Crenshaw shopping mall crowded with Black, Mexican, Central American, and Salvadoran families and their children, I see signs of what Wacquant and Wilson call hyperghettoization. Now this extreme concentration of economically deprived people is no longer confined to one racial group; today, minority groups live next door to one another in segregated neighborhoods where more than 50 percent of kids drop out of high school and where gang violence had steadily increased. Most of these families, squeezed into small and tattered neighborhoods, live next door to strangers who do not speak their language or know their cultural ways.

Since 1990, nearly one-third of these families have been living below the poverty line, mere miles from some of Los Angeles's wealthiest neighborhoods. Those with jobs work as janitors, housekeepers, gardeners, or child care providers—all low-wage jobs. Most of these children attend poorly funded schools; more than half of the kids enrolled are taught by unqualified or substitute teachers; the rest have dropped out of school altogether.

Most of the restaurants in this area consist of fast-food places like McDonald's or Burger King, which some health professionals claim contribute to the high percentage of diabetes and obesity among inner-city minority kids.[28] Some people buy their wares at the mom-and-pop stores that dot the strip malls. Some of the kids' parents complain that these stores are so bereft of quality clothing and food that most people (if they have transportation and can afford it) travel thirty miles outside their neighborhoods to shop and eat at malls in Century City, Huntington Beach, or Glendale. Ralphs, one of three chain supermarkets in the area, is guarded by turnstiles so that people's movements in and out of the store can be monitored by security cameras. The price of food in these supermarkets is at least five to ten cents higher than in stores in nearby Venice or Santa Monica. The USC students tell me that they purchase only canned goods from these stores; "the fresh food doesn't look so good," Theresa says.

South Central is also home to fifty thousand residents, some of whom live in well-tended neighborhoods. I drive down pleasant streets where large family homes stand in the shade of large eucalyptus trees. I pass mom-and-pop stores with painted Spanish signs and weathered but tidy homes with low chain-link fences, scrappy dogs, and statues of Jesus and the Virgin Mary. I see large mural signs everywhere. On some streets, the murals are marked with graffiti.

In contrast to the pleasant side streets, the commercial boulevards of Florence and Normandie catch my eye. These areas are both economically and psychologically depressing. They are dominated by unprepossessing establishments doing a desultory business in hair and nail care, party supplies, burglar alarms, and auto parts and small storefront churches.

Much of the entrepreneurial energy of the neighborhood goes into religion. In one stretch of five storefronts, four are tiny Black churches. One church has a large sign on its roof depicting a group of Black men carrying a coffin: "Will It Take Six Strong Men to Bring You Back to Church?" I pass a blank billboard and remember the recent protest by a group of parents against a billboard promoting a movie based on the life of rapper 50 Cent. The distributors of the *Get Rich or Die Tryin'* billboard, picturing the muscular rapper holding a gun in his left hand and a microphone in his right, complied with parents' wishes and removed the billboard.[29]

∎   ∎   ∎

Today, an extensive underground economy in South Central Los Angeles revolves around the manufacture and distribution of illicit drugs. Drug trafficking has contributed to a critical level of gang- and non-gang-related violence. In some neighborhoods, a variety of businesses play a role in the drug industry, such as automobile towing companies, automobile dealerships, and fictitious businesses serving as fronts for the sale of cocaine. Liquor stores also play a role in the overall picture of both drug trafficking and drug use.

In many South Central Los Angeles neighborhoods, small off-sale alcohol outlets or "corner stores" act as magnets for a variety of substance abuse problems. Loitering, public drunkenness, public urination, gambling, prostitution, and drug dealing characterize the environment around many problem locations. Many of the kids say that when they go to these corner stores to buy sodas and "junk" to eat, they often encounter the neighborhood drunks buying cheap wine or panhandling or gambling in front of the stores or on nearby streets.

In addition, customers meet the dealers at the stores to make their transactions. In many instances, such "problem store" environments lead to violence and leave neighborhood residents exposed to potential harm when they go out to buy food or other items also available at the corner stores.

There are no major furniture stores within twenty or twenty-five miles of South Central. The Macy's department store on Crenshaw Boulevard and a Walmart are the only major department stores in the area. Several parents point to both stores as selling inferior merchandise, especially the Macy's in Baldwin Hills, according to an NAI parent: "You expect Walmart to carry cheap products, but Macy's?" She shakes her head. Also, South Central does not have sufficient health care services.

The Watts and Rodney King riots may seem to set South Central apart from other communities, but some consider the Martin Luther King, Jr./Charles R. Drew hospital scandal the most tragic story of all. The hospital was built after the 1965 Watts Riots to bring health care to poor minority communities in south Los Angeles. King/Drew was supposed to provide a valuable service to a community that, until the early 1970s, did not have a hospital to serve its residents.

In 2007, King/Drew—a hospital with such a notorious reputation that its residents referred to it as "Killer King"[30]—closed. Entire departments were found to be riddled with incompetence, internal strife, and, in some cases, criminality. Employees had pilfered and sometimes sold the hospital's drugs, chronic absenteeism was rampant, and assaults between hospital workers were not uncommon. Despite King/Drew's repeated promises to regulators, the problems went unresolved for years.[31]

The hospital had been plagued by patient deaths resulting from sloppy nursing care, among other things. The county tried over several years to correct the problems, putting millions of dollars into disciplining workers, reorganizing management, closing the trauma unit, and reducing the number of beds from two hundred to forty-eight.[32] Many of the residents had a grand time laughing at stories of a stroke patient who had to wait nearly five hours for a drug to help prevent heart attacks and recurring strokes. At one point, pharmacists would not fill the order because a doctor had misspelled the name of the drug. But the final blow that led to King/Drew's closure had to do with the death of Edith Isabel Rodriguez, who was found bleeding from the mouth and had been writhing in pain for forty-five minutes in a hospital waiting area. Experts have said she could have survived had she been treated early enough.[33]

Other stories include that of a paraplegic with a pressure sore and bone infection who was not given a laxative suppository that had been ordered and reordered by a physician over at least five days. Or the inspector who noted errors in three of six medications given to a patient. Or, in the case of a tuberculosis patient, an inspector who found a missing dose of intravenous

antibiotics on a pharmacy counter more than two hours after it had been ordered, with a sticker that read "missing dose." Everyone I interviewed knew
of someone who needed hospital care but refused it when they found out
they would have to go to King/Drew. Everyone especially laughed about the
stories of area police who needed hospital care for injuries suffered on duty
but who refused to go to "Killer King." Although King/Drew opened in
1972 with the promise that it would be "the very best hospital in America,"
it became, by various measures, one of the worst. It paid out more per patient
for medical malpractice than any of the state's seventeen other public hospi-
tals or the six University of California medical centers.[34]

The laughter always stops when I bring up the point that closing King/
Drew means that more than forty-seven thousand critically ill patients a
year have to find another hospital—most likely, USC Medical Center—to
serve them.[35] But residents are impressed with the idea that King/Drew's
emergency room gained some fame for training doctors who were on their
way to Iraq. Their reason for training there? They had the opportunity to
work on gang members and others who had been shot or suffered from related problems that were typically faced by doctors in Iraq.[36]

• • •

I see the deterioration, the hyperghettoization that Wacquant and Wilson
refer to, as I drive through nearby neighborhood streets occupied by single-
family homes and small apartment buildings with wrought-iron security
grids covering doors and windows.[37] I do not see places for kids to have fun
skateboarding or playing basketball on the streets. Nor do I see adults walking their dogs or sitting outside their homes enjoying the spring air. They
are certainly not picnicking or playing basketball at the two parks in the
area, both known as hangouts for gangs like the notorious Rollin' 60s or
Mara Salvatrucha (MS-13). The "old heads" who could watch over the children of South Central as the men did in Anderson's ethnography about
Philadelphia's inner-city men in South Central are mostly in prison or have
been killed in gang battles.

According to a travel guide, tourists are warned that South Central has
long had a reputation for violence.[38] It was the scene of the 1992 L.A. riots
and is known for producing the Bloods, the Crips, and other notorious gangs.
The travel guide notes, "Murders are so common in this area that a study of a
4-mile radius around 108th and Normandie showed 407 murders since 2007.
Regardless of whether or not you are driving, going to this area is just a bad
idea. Less flashy cars will attract more of the wrong kind of attention."[39]

Few outsiders venture into South Central, except, of course, those connected with USC. You do not drive into the South Central area unless you are a resident, attend or work at the university, or are one of a small number of faculty members who have taken advantage of the faculty housing program and live near the campus. That drive certainly illustrates the great disconnect between the economic situation of the middle class who live close to the USC campus and the average inner-city residents. For the most part, few college students and inner-city kids socialize.

At the corner of East Fifty-First Street, as I wait for a light to change, two women in extreme miniskirts walk down the sidewalk alongside two rough-looking men. I check the car doors—in case I need to escape—and feel ashamed of the fear, but the kids I interview cannot escape, and so I drive on. I recall Barack Obama's argument that although people of color have come a long way since the civil rights movement, there is still the emotional reaction to the past: "Even after the laws were passed and lynching ceased, the closest thing to freedom would still involve escape, emotional if not physical, away from ourselves, away from what we knew."[40]

Some things are changing. Despite the gang violence in one South Central neighborhood, civic leaders have brought about numerous improvements, including a resurfacing of a basketball court and new bullet-resistant lights.[41] The author of a recent newspaper article writes that the community is doing whatever it can to bring money into South Central: "Activists hope to use money from bus tours for community good." After a VIP preview last weekend, L.A. Gang Tours expects to open to the public in January, giving tourists a look at the cradle of the nation's gang culture—the birthplace of many of the city's gangs, including the Crips, the Bloods, Florence 13, and 18th Street.[42]

I talk to Annie Jordon, whose son is in NAI, about the tour. "What's that gonna do?" she says. "In South Central, there are no jobs, not here; they have no money to move away from their troubles. This is South Central."

■　■　■

The South Central kids interviewed in this book seem to agree with Annie Jordon. They demonstrate an incredible knowledge of outdated social theories and a willingness to share their perspectives on their histories, values, and plans. We see through their eyes what it means to live in a socially isolated community where, as Wilson argues, "concentrated poverty adversely affects one's changes in life, beginning in early childhood and adolescence."[43]

4 |

"Send Them All to Iraq"

F ew people seem to care about the fears of kids like those of South Central. Instead, many Americans agree with the "ghetto thug" stereotype of them. One blogger, writing about South Central kids, complains, "They don't have the tools to process what they are doing to their community. All they know is Murder, Death, and Kill. Send them all to Iraq."[1] I can recall quite vividly an acquaintance telling me, in reference to the election of President Barack Obama, "Now these thugs have no excuse; since President Obama's election, they can't blame skin color." These views are not surprising. They fall in line with the general perception of the urban inner-city kid. After all, these views are embedded in the American ideology of individualism and in the unsupported assumption that all inner-city kids are petty criminals and products of families out of touch with mainstream values.

In fact, the powerful image of Black and Latino middle schoolers as "ghetto thugs" or "ghetto types" has captured the attention of many Americans, including those who live in the inner city. In the case of the ghetto thug—an image constructed and imposed by "outsiders"—it serves as a model for drive-by shootings, rising school dropout rates, and the deterioration of the inner city. Patricia Hill Collins would argue that while these images are false, like all cultural images they weave a powerful spell over the minds of everyone, even the young people who are often unaware of the power of such imagery. She has argued that images we have of others can control our perceptions and therefore come to define a person's identity and determine what is acceptable and unacceptable.[2] One reason these images work so well is that they are supported by an even more powerful notion that most Americans have of themselves—the deeply embedded belief in the primary importance of the individual and in the virtues of self-reliance, hard work, and personal independence.

■ ■ ■

Historian and writer James Truslow Adams, who coined the term *American Dream* in his 1931 book *Epic of America*, writes, "The American Dream is that dream of a land in which life should be better and richer and fuller for everyone, with opportunity for each according to ability or achievement . . . [a dream] of social order in which each man and each woman shall be able to attain to the fullest stature of which they are innately capable, and be recognized by others for what they are, regardless of the fortuitous circumstances of birth or position."[3] The view of the American Dream as the product of individual hard work has been used as a benchmark in identifying such problems as high dropout rates and gang violence as dysfunctional.

We all know the Horatio Alger stories of the poor who move up the ladder of success. And it is true that a few people of color, born into poverty, through their ability to perform extremely hard labor, acquire some wealth. We hear over and over the stories of popular celebrities such as Oprah Winfrey and Jennifer Lopez who overcome poverty and inner-city influences. I recall a Colombian-born woman boasting to me that through hard work as a domestic worker, she saved enough money to invest in a real estate firm. "It is possible for a Latina like me to become rich," she claimed. "If I can do it, so can anyone else." In this Latina's version of the American Dream, regardless of social class or circumstances of birth, with hard work, as Adams put it, "life should be better and richer and fuller."

Is that dream still possible? Today most Americans, including a large population of Blacks and Latinos, do not think so, given that many—both the middle class and the poor—are finding themselves on the unemployment line because of the recent economic recession.[4]

We also learn from the kids that no matter how hard they try, and while most are doing well in school, the label of *dysfunctional* means that others will always see them as not worthy of attaining the American Dream. As one person put it to me, "That is all the city will let them be. Everywhere they go, someone's reminding them that they're racial outsiders."

These kids may be "racial outsiders" to some, but to others, they are held responsible for the socioeconomic state of their communities. In May 2006, on the NAACP's anniversary observance of *Brown v. Board of Education*, comedian Bill Cosby, insisting that the American Dream is still accessible to all people of color, criticized poor and lower-middle-class Blacks for poor parenting, rampant out-of-wedlock births, and high dropout and crime rates. "People who struggled to gain civil rights marched and were hit in the face with rocks and punched in the face to get an education," Cosby said at the time. "And we've got these knuckleheads walking around who don't want to learn English. They don't want to accept that they have to study to get an education." He later explained that he had been motivated to speak out after an eight-year-old girl was killed in her aunt's living room during a drive-by shooting.[5]

The crowd responded enthusiastically, not only to Cosby but also to the panel that joined him on the program, including Jesse Jackson, NAACP president Kweisi Mfume, educators, legal experts, and a mother of adopted and foster children. His message played to the crowd's fear of the "ghetto thug" myth and to the educators' and others' lack of insight into institutional arrangements that permitted these problems to occur in the first place. Others excoriated him; civil rights leaders denounced Cosby as elitist, mean-spirited, and out of touch with young people and the poor.

Nowhere in his indictment of inner-city kids and their parents does Cosby consider that his view of the American Dream fails to examine those the social factors that militate against the assumption of equal opportunity—primarily the long history of imposed segregation, job discrimination, institutional disrespect and disregard, and "police brutality," as described by João Helion Costa Vargas in his ethnography of South Central.[6] Cosby's view also does not consider the degree to which these kids are part of a vicious cycle, in which, as George Lipsitz argues, people (in this case, middle schoolers) have to struggle to survive policies of racial segregation and the prospect of no future.[7] Nor does Cosby's view consider the extent to which stereotypes—for example, "low-class thugs" who "trade school for prison"—act, according to sociologist Victor Rios, to criminalize youth at an early age, thereby maintaining their low social status.[8]

Cosby's argument raises a question: Who will want to hire these inner-city kids? This negative attitude blames drive-by shootings and kids' low graduation rates on the kids themselves or on their families. Ignored are the economic and social conditions that contribute to high rates of violence and dropouts. Also ignored are kids who do not belong to gangs and, like the kids in this study, want to grow up like other teenagers.

To isolate one factor—the individual person or family—as the cause of the condition they find themselves in, in this case the culture of poverty, creates a two-part dilemma: (1) the closed, self-perpetuating system discussed previously and, (2) following from the first, an unrealistic expectation of individual responsibility for a much larger and more complicated problem. One person, one family, without access to the good life, would be hard put to heroically improve poor school quality, upgrade the general run-down condition of crowded neighborhoods, and gain the respect and protection of local police.

The Culture-of-Poverty Approach

The culture-of-poverty perspective has a long and often protected history in the United States, implicated as it is in a polarized class structure, loosely shielded by an ineffectual notion of "social equity" and closely guarded from close examination by the ever-vague American success story. College students, including those in this study, learn that an elusive "social equality" is an integral feature of correctness and "success." It follows in some minds that inner-city kids unable to attain those goals do not process the kinds of values needed to move out of a vicious cycle, placing them outside definition—unsuccessful, incorrect. Invisible.

According to this scenario, they are likely to remain poor because their culture deviates from the norm. Therefore, the poor lack an ethic of work, school achievement, and family tradition. The implied assumption is that until inner-city kids change their culture, no amount of government or societal intervention will motivate the poor to adopt the values of mainstream culture. Yet despite widespread belief in this notion, the data prove otherwise: inner-city kids attend poorly funded schools in segregated areas, where their parents either are unemployed or earn low wages.[9]

By placing responsibility for inner-city crime on kids, the culture of poverty avoids taking responsibility for larger, more basic structural issues such as the poor quality of most inner-city schools, the general run-down condition of crowded neighborhoods, the poor response of the police to criminal activity in these neighborhoods, and, as reported by most of the kids, the general feeling of being exposed to but not protected from the violence they see on a daily basis.

Furthermore, the culture-of-poverty approach, by polarizing successful and poor, ignores the experiences of kids, especially those of color, within their real-world context of contemporary race, ethnic, and class inequalities. The culture-of-poverty view, in a circular argument, allows the college students in this study to ignore the insidious use of "social equality" as an integral feature of correctness and "success." It follows that inner-city kids who have not attained that status are perceived as worthless, unable to move out of a vicious cycle. In other words, these kids will not or cannot bridge that gap.

The Oppositional Culture Theory

By focusing on the deficits of individuals living outside the American Dream, the culture of poverty fails to account for broader societal structures and historical processes. John Ogbu argues that kids have learned how to respond to the problems they face in their communities by developing what he calls "oppositional culture."[10] He argues that minorities develop a defiant attitude about mainstream culture and feel alienated from schools, learning, and education. He claims, for example, that studying hard and excelling in school are devalued by minorities as culturally illegitimate. They tend to develop a collective oppositional culture, a frame of reference that actively rejects mainstream behaviors to undermine academic achievement.[11]

Ogbu uses the idea of involuntary minorities. He observed that in some cases, groups of people of the same race but located in different countries manifested different ability and/or achievement levels according to some measures. He studied how, why, and to what degree this might be so. He concluded that Americans could be divided into "voluntary minorities" (groups of immigrants who chose to come to the United States and their descendants) versus "involuntary" or "caste-like" minorities (descendants of groups who found themselves in the United States, or under U.S. jurisdiction, against their will).[12]

Ogbu argues that involuntary minorities often adopted an "oppositional identity" to the mainstream culture in response to a glass ceiling imposed or maintained by White society on the job success of their parents and others in their communities.[13] Therefore, he reasoned, some non-Whites "failed to observe the link between educational achievement and access to jobs."[14]

A predominantly Black high school in a low-income area of Washington, D.C., had what Ogbu said was an "oppositional culture," in which Black youth dismissed academically oriented behavior as "white."[15] In another

study, when Angela Neal-Barnett asked students in a focus group to identify "acting white" behavior, they listed actions such as speaking standard
English, enrolling in an advanced placement (AP) or honors class, wearing
clothes from the Gap or Abercrombie and Fitch (instead of Tommy Hilfiger
or FUBU), and wearing shorts in the winter.[16]

In the late 1990s, Ogbu found much the same thing in quite another
setting, an upper-class suburb of Cleveland, Ohio, called Shaker Heights.[17]
Although that city had been integrated for generations, large racial disparities in achievement persisted. When Ogbu detected an anti-intellectual culture among Blacks in the local high school, Shaker Heights, that culture
became virtually synonymous with the problem of "acting white."

Ogbu traced the roots of the "oppositional culture" to institutionalized
racism within American society, which he contends led Blacks to define academic achievement as the prerogative of Whites and to invest themselves
instead in alternative pursuits.[18] Other observers, however, place the blame
for "acting white" squarely on the shoulders of Blacks. In one article, writer
John McWhorter, for example, argues that anti-intellectualism, separat-
ism, and a self-perpetuated identity of victimhood are factors limiting Black
Americans as a group.[19] These two theories, the former blaming "acting
white" on a racist society and the latter blaming social problems in the Black
community on a self-imposed cultural sabotage, have emerged as the pre-
dominant explanations for disavowing mainstream cultural norms among
American Blacks.

Although Ogbu's conclusions have gained support, a later study ob-
tained different results. In fact, African American students are hardly the
only group to avoid academic work. In James Coleman's 1933 classic work
The Adolescent Society, members of a school's sports teams and cheerlead-
ers were the most popular students in public schools. Coleman argues that
students in general, not just Black students, tend to focus more attention
on sports than on academics.[20] Other ethnographers have found variations
on "acting white" among the Buraku outcasts of Japan, Italian immigrants
in Boston's West End, the Maori of New Zealand, and the British working
class, among others.[21] In 2003, Karolyn Tyson directed an eighteen-month
study at eleven North Carolina schools and found that White and Black
students have essentially the same attitudes about scholastic achievement:
students in both groups want to succeed in school, and they show higher
levels of self-esteem when they do better in school.[22]

However, some studies do show that some Latino and Black kids engage
in labeling other students as "acting white," as a criticism of their efforts to

advance academically.[23] On the basis of my personal experiences with Black teenagers, I suggest that unlike the "ghetto type" image, this stereotype appears to be self-inflicted. In a way, "acting white" has become another controlling image that Black kids have to confront.

Claude Steele and Joshua Aronson's theory of stereotype threat suggests that a person's social identity, which he or she defines as group membership in categories defined by age, gender, religion, and ethnicity, has significance when rooted in concrete situations.[24] Steele and Aronson define these situations as identity contingencies—settings in which a person is treated according to a specific social identity. They argue that when a person's social identity is attached to a negative stereotype, he or she will tend to underperform in a manner consistent with that stereotype.[25] The NAI kids did not appear to be caught up in the "acting white" phenomenon. According to William Tierney and Alexander Jun's study of NAI, the program put a great deal of effort into building up positive cultural integrity. This positive cultural integrity encompasses the students self-labeling as "scholars" and completion and success in schoolwork as being a positive thing to be praised for.[26]

Tierney and Jun's study examines the idea that including families and neighborhoods in the context of students' learning builds up positive cultural integrity so that better outcomes will be achieved. Reconciling the students' environment with their schooling creates more positive concepts of self-image. For example, the authors argue that "NAI affirms local contexts and enables adolescents to develop positive conceptions of their neighborhood rather than assume that to succeed in education they must change who they are."[27]

To go even further, NAI seeks to disrupt what it calls "tracking"—essentially school administrators and teachers determining students' future achievement and priming them for that outcome—by showing them future options. Tracking helps teachers place students into different learning pathways (such as academic honors or remedial work) in their academic life, theoretically in order to serve their academic needs better.[28] USC has played a role in opening up future possibilities for kids by offering a full need-based scholarship to students who graduate from NAI and earn acceptance at USC. The Willard kids who did not have access to NAI's kind of support system spoke of wanting to achieve educationally, but sadly, some told stories of peers who accused them of "acting white."

Steele and Aronson's study further ties underperformance to the person's anxiety that he or she will conform to the negative stereotype.[29] That anxiety manifests itself in various ways, including distraction and increased body temperature, all of which diminish performance level. Willard kids DeWayne, J.D., and Nace mention getting into fights, and DeWayne seems more focused on his modeling career than advancing his school performance. Low expectations of teachers and other adults reinforce the idea that these kids are unable to do well in school, thereby reinforcing the idea that they are dumb, and thus they react by taking an oppositional stance to school achievement, as Ogbu argues. But this kind of attitude could well be a response to deep feelings of inferiority, as Steele and Aronson suggest.

Steele and Aronson make clear that stereotype threat is not limited to historically disadvantaged groups and that every person endures stereotype threat in certain contexts. For example, they cite a study testing stereotype threat among White engineering students. When the White students took a test after being told that Asians typically outperformed Whites on that test, the Whites performed significantly worse than they would have otherwise.[30]

Steele and Aronson's message is not without hope. They stress that abilities are expandable and that there is no truth to allegations that a particular group lacks a particular capacity[31]—as the NAI kids demonstrate. In a study examining the significations of stereotype threat on women participants, Paul Davis, Steven Spencer, and Claude Steele maintain that stereotype threat will continue as a default setting until steps are taken to counteract it. Above all, the authors argue that at an institutional level, "it is possible to create leadership environments (i.e., identity-safe environments)." They go on to say, "These identity-safe environments enable stigmatized individuals to enter previously threatening situations without the risk of being personally reduced to a negative stereotype targeting their social identity."[32] The notion of an identity-safe environment implies that efforts have to be taken to establish that diverse social identities add integral value to a setting. I suggest that diverse social identities add integral value to our relationships with others, as we see when the kids introduce us to photos of their "fake" family members.

This dilemma, borne out in my conversations with the USC students and the NAI kids, speaks to larger structural issues, as discussed in Michael Schwalbe's *Rigging the Game: How Inequality Is Reproduced in Everyday Life*. Schwalbe argues that "we need to look at the laws, policies, and routine procedures that allow some people to control others [for example, the kids studied for this book] and to exploit them in various ways." Schwalbe further states, "It is these laws, policies, and procedures—what I refer to as rules of the game—that allow some people to have more resources than others."[33] By *rules of the game*, he means "the ideas people share about what can and can't be done without making trouble for themselves and others. If we go too far in breaking those rules, we can be thrown out of the situation or locked up. While rules don't literally force us to do anything, they can compel certain kinds of behavior and outcomes."[34]

Schwalbe argues that rules, policies, and procedures operate to benefit some groups at the expense of others. Rules can make the perpetuation of inequality seem like an impersonal process. For example, Cosby and others blame the kids (and parents) but not the rules, laws, and procedures that keep them trapped in their social conditions, perpetuating their social problems, such as the negative image of Black and Latino kids and, in this case, the laws and procedures of the educational system and the larger society that reinforce that stereotype.

Never mind Cosby's total disregard for the social forces hammering down the inner city. Most of his audience agrees with him, holding these kids responsible for South Central's social problems. Perhaps the space between the lives of South Central kids and Cosby's middle-class background is too large to see otherwise. Perhaps the largely Black audience needs to believe in the American Dream just like other Americans. Or perhaps this audience believes that blaming inner-city kids and their parents for their community's problems is a requirement for those who need to assimilate into mainstream America, which means conforming to values and ideologies promoting a willingness to imitate, to follow, to obey, or, to use a popular cliché, to "toe the line." Or perhaps Cosby's comments prove sociologist C. Wright Mills's observation that some (in this case, Cosby) who are critical of others "can slip past structure to focus on isolated situations" and think of problems as "problems of individuals."[35] Can Mills's position be brought to bear on questions concerning whether individual achievement is even possible under current social conditions in South Central?

According to sociologist Pierre Bourdieu, a lower-class child growing up in an environment where success is rare is much less likely to develop strong ambitions than is a middle-class boy or girl growing up in a social world peopled by those who have attained educational success.[36] Bourdieu's theory of achievement also raises significant questions for this research: Can an inner-city child aspire to achieve and transcend the limitations of his or her objective probabilities?

On the one hand, if Kyle manages to get into college, he will have a chance to acquire both cultural capital and social capital and perhaps break his family's cycle of poverty. As Schwalbe points out, these forms of capital are elements of processes that unfold over time: "They're part of the processes whereby some people get ahead and most don't. So, if we want to understand how inequality is perpetuated, it's useful to look at how these forms of capital are distributed and how people are able or not able to use them to get some kind of payoff. They're part of the processes whereby some people get ahead and most don't."[37] The question I ask, after reading Cosby's statement, has to do with whether these stereotypes conform to the actual experiences of all inner-city kids. Cosby's statements condemning inner-city kids and their parents have helped me gain a more profound understanding of the poverty of these inner-city kids' relationships with an authority figure like Cosby, who as an adult could use his voice to support them. Instead, Cosby chooses to rely on common but unexamined perceptions and in doing so further isolates the kids from receiving support from many in their own communities.

III

Kids' School Stories

5 |

Teachers and Dirty Bathrooms

"I Want to Show You My School"

Abby, a pretty, petite fourteen-year-old African American wearing a white short-sleeve blouse and blue striped short pants flashes a big smile as she sits down at the classroom table. Abby was in the fourth grade when her mother received a call from her daughter's teacher and an NAI staff member recommending her daughter for the NAI tutorial program. She was excited at first. The staff warned her that she would have to work hard, keep up with her regular schoolwork, attend tutoring classes three times a week, and finish all of the extra assignments required by NAI. And she would also have to attend academic classes at 9:00 A.M. on Saturday mornings. She began to worry. What about her play time? She was not sure she could give it up.

NAI's After-School Support System

Now Abby attends Jefferson, a high school in South Central that is considered to be among the lowest performing in the Los Angeles Unified School District.[1] Most of the non-NAI students at these schools are a class or two behind NAI students. Still, Abby admits that she has to work hard to stay in the program. According to NAI director Kim Thomas-Barrios, Abby's parents make her stay in the program. But that can be difficult because, as the director explains to me, "The biggest obstacle can be the home situation.

Most of these kids are from families who do not have a high school or college background themselves and, therefore, may need their kids to help out with family chores." According to Thomas-Barrios, "They may be responsible for child care—babysitting all night—household chores, dinner service, and cleanup work." The director attributes this way of thinking to the notion that "these parents don't see themselves in the bigger picture as parents of college-bound kids. And other parents may not trust the system. That is, they may not believe their kids need to spend time studying or that it will result in getting them into USC."

Most of these kids, like Abby, struggle to balance the demands of NAI classwork with those of their other classes. Some, the director points out, "are not ready to do the work. If they leave the program, they can't come back since the program demands a commitment of at least four years." Twelve-year-olds Fantasia and Sandee, whose interviews appear in Chapter 9, drop out of school and the NAI program.

Most, who stay, like Abby and Kyle, agree with Cesar, who says he is "sweating" his way through schoolwork and the weekly twelve-hour tutorial classes. Abby may be working hard, but she would not trade places with the non-NAI students she sees at Jefferson High. She likes the emotional support she receives from NAI staff, who help whenever and in whatever way they can, if they need to, by talking to school administrators about classwork or unsupportive teachers. NAI also offers psychological counseling for kids and parents to help them cope with issues such as having to end old friendships, especially if those friends are involved in gangs, and to learn how to form friendships with other NAI kids.

The staff also offers support to parents by helping them become more involved in kids' schoolwork or dealing with gossip or bad news that can be discouraging if not handled right away. The ability to receive tutoring help may not have been enough to prevent Fantasia and Sandee (Chapter 9) from dropping out, but that support does seem to give most NAI kids a strong sense of confidence that they can do well in school.

The Willard After-School Center's Support System

Another African American kid, fourteen-year-old J.D., a small diamond-shaped earring in his right earlobe, wearing a loose-fitting white T-shirt that hangs to the knees of his black jeans, has a great deal to say about his high school. J.D. attends Willard's after-school center and likes the homework help he receives whenever he can "drag [him]self" to the center. His biggest problem? "Going to that dumb school," he says, pointing to a picture of a three-story school building (see Figure 5.1), a traditional urban school model, larger and more ornate in design than the brown square box of Abby's prefab, a design considered to be an affordable way to house the growing student population (see Figure 5.2).

Those schools may be affordable, but according to a number of recent studies, students like J.D. pay a huge price in terms of their health. According to one report, these buildings are built with "toxic material" and have poor ventilation, which increases health risks for students and teachers. The report also reveals that 27 percent of California teachers report problems with cockroaches, rats, or mice, and 17 percent of them complain that the bathrooms at their schools are "either dirty or closed."[2]

Sadly, California's educational system suffers from far worse problems than ventilation and rodent troubles. According to a report by the Rand Corporation, in 2005, the California public school system lagged behind most of the nation, ranking above only Louisiana on almost every objective measurement of student achievement, funding, teacher qualifications, and school facilities. For instance, California school districts receive low levels of funds compared to other states, and a "substantial portion of California's teachers are not fully qualified or board certified."[3]

Figure 5.1

Figure 5.2

In fact, in 2000, on the anniversary of the *Brown v. Board of Education* ruling, American Civil Liberties Union (ACLU) lawyers filed a class-action lawsuit charging that the state of California had failed to provide even a basic education to low-income students.[4] According to the report, students at Jefferson High School in South Central do not have enough books to take home to study, and teachers missed many days, which means that substitutes are heavily relied on as long-term teachers.[5] In an article titled "Los Angeles Schools: Hobbled and Hurting," published in 1993 and reprinted in 2008, the author calls the Los Angeles public school system "a stricken giant, hobbled by financial problems, a threatened teachers strike and racial and ethnic strife." Furthermore, the author concludes, "overcrowded classrooms, leaky roofs, outdated textbooks, metal detectors and police officers patrolling schools are common in America's inner-city schools."[6]

J.D. and other kids who attend the Willard Center seem to lack Abby's sense of confidence, which perhaps has to do with NAI's ability to dramatically affect kids' lives, although Willard's staff seems as dedicated to them as NAI's staff. In fact, Willard's pamphlet touts the center as a source of hope and service to low-income youth. Willard's director, Marge Whiting, greets me warmly when I arrive. She walks me around five rooms filled with various games and books. She and the other staff express a great deal of support for the kids. They seem to feel obligated to provide a supportive environment where the kids will feel welcomed; as Whiting puts it, "These kids will just hang out in the street if we didn't provide these services. There are enough minority kids doing that already." Of course, Willard, a publicly funded program, cannot offer kids tutorial classes, although it does offer assistance with homework; it also cannot contract with kids' parents to make the kids' seek homework assistance. J.D. and the other Willard kids can come and go as they please.

But here the differences between NAI and Willard programs end. Although the NAI kids can ask the staff to talk with school administrators and teachers about student problems, it may not help—as you will see. Both NAI and Willard kids have what Abby calls "a ton of pictures" and stories about rodents, leaky toilets, disgruntled teachers, and other school problems. In fact, all fifty-four kids eagerly revealed what they see as a deeply flawed inner-city school system.

School Colors

"I wanted to show you my friends." Abby points to a photo of NAI kids posing for her picture. I am struck by the scene. The photo shows the group of about twenty kids, all wearing white T-shirts. Several are displaying what appear to be gang signs. At first glance, I think I see the group imitate a gang pose. (See Figure 5.3.)

After I took a second look, and based on the kids' discussions of these photos, I realized that what we see in the photo are signs that the gangs' culture has gained a tremendous hold on the cultural life of South Central kids. Indeed, the photo is telling us that the kids, who later say how much they are deadly afraid of the gangs, also understand that culture and that to some degree they may find at least the gang signs glamorous and provocative—giving them a feeling of machismo; after all, they are twelve-to-fifteen-year-old kids.

They are also telling us that the gang culture so dominates inner-city life that everyone in this community knows that they can suffer the consequences of not adhering to its dictates, for example, wearing the right colors. In their neighborhood, wearing the wrong color T-shirt—the Crips' gang color blue or the Bloods' color red—means being mistaken by the rival gang as a member of the other gang, and they can be beaten or killed. To avoid

Figure 5.3

that problem, until recently, most kids not affiliated with gangs would wear white, a neutral color. However, the gangs learn quickly; to hide gang affiliations, they also wear white T-shirts and other neutral colors.[7]

Being involved in a gang is a "no-no," Abby tells me when I ask about the group hand signs. NAI's contract stipulates that she will be disqualified from the program if she associates with anyone, including friends, who are gang members. Twelve-year-old Martino, who receives help with his math homework at the Willard Center, says he has to stay away from old friends who are destructive to him. "I just keep to myself. I say hi, and they say hi. But it's not talking. Sometimes I have to deal with gangs that roam near my school. But I just walk fast way far away from them." Martino may say he can walk away, but the kids' photos say that the gangs' ability to reign over South Central creates a highly toxic environment for them.

The Kids Have Their Say about the Schools They Attend

The stress is clear in Abby's tone of voice when she talks about the troubles at her school. "See, in this picture, that's my friend who had to get to class. She's late. She has to wait in that nasty room for someone to escort her to class. We hate that school." (See Figure 5.4.)

Figure 5.4

Cesar, a tall, chubby twelve-year-old eighth grader with a sly smile, has photos of his friend Juan standing in front of a prefab building bordered by a chain-link fence (see Figure 5.5). I ask, "Cesar, why did you take this photo? Anything stand out?" He replies softly, "It's the back of my school. I don't like that building. They have things in the building that they don't like to put to use. Like they have lockers, but [they don't use them because] they're afraid of us because the sixth graders—everybody destroyed [them]."

EK: How does that make you feel that you can't use your lockers?
CESAR: Maybe they don't trust us. And we're not responsible.
EK: You have to carry a lot of books around?
CESAR: We can't put anything down at all during the day.[8] And when you dress for P.E., you just barely change and the teacher is already counting to ten, so you have to get out. And there are rats. I saw one coming out of the cafeteria and going into the trash. Can you believe in the cafeteria, where there is our food?
EK: So, do you eat in the cafeteria?
CESAR: No. I don't, and I am starving. Most of the eighth grade don't eat there. We snack. This guy name Miguel, he says his stomach

Figure 5.5

hurts, and he will be like, "This is nasty" but will keep on eating the food. Ugh. [*His voice sags.*] No one cares.

Stories of trust and responsibility echo throughout these discussions.

The Bathroom Facilities

Only Jessica, Sharon, and Cesar take photos of their school bathrooms. Jessica, a petite twelve-year-old African American, flips through her photos. She pulls out a photo showing an unflushed toilet in front of a wall marked by dirt spots—what she calls the "filthy bathroom and unflushed toilet at my school" (see Figure 5.6).

From my middle-class adult perch, when I see this photo I think Jessica is having a laugh on me. After all, they are kids; why should they care about this project? Eighth grader Jessica, slender with a dimpled, round face and quiet demeanor, sits across from me in my office on campus, the tall chair making her look tiny and younger than her age. But she is not shy about her school's bathroom conditions. "Look at what we have to put up with. We get blamed for this, but nobody cleans it up."

Figure 5.6

At that moment, her voice rises as she pushes her shoulders up as if to give more strength to her statement. At first, I am amused by the indignation of this twelve-year-old. But her photos and comments, it turns out, reflect a larger story about South Central's infrastructure than the three photographs convey and are not limited to Jessica's school. I ask other kids a general question about their school:

EK: Anything you would change about your school?
CESAR: The bathrooms. They're messy, they dirty, they stink.
EK: So, how does that feel when you have to go to the bathroom?
CESAR: I don't. Yeah. So I don't want to drink too much water. And there's no toilet paper in the bathrooms. And the janitors won't give you any, if you ask. They're just standing around talking. They don't care. Like literally when I have to go to the bathroom, I have to, like, pull my pants up because otherwise I would get everything wet. And sometimes there's tagging on the walls. That means they clean up outside but not in the bathrooms. And there would not be toilet paper.

EK: What kind of message do you get when you see the bathrooms
in that condition?

CESAR: Only go when there is an emergency. [*Everyone laughs.*]

These bathroom stories are not just the figments of these kids' imagination. These conditions are, in fact, quite common in inner-city schools.
According to the complaint filed in the ACLU lawsuit mentioned previously, inner-city bathrooms like those at Jessica's Jefferson High do not have
basic supplies such as toilet paper, running water, and soap, and the toilets
are always backed up or overflowing. The floors are often "wet and sticky
and . . . smell of human waste."[9]

All the kids who see Jessica's photograph begin to talk about being frus-
trated by the lack of attention paid to their "ugly bathrooms" complaints.
Jessica lowers her voice as if we are not alone in the classroom: "I go when
I get home. But it's not good to hold it for that long." Jessica says that her
mother has warned her little brother to "wait until he comes home for lunch.
Don't go unless it's an emergency."

Fourteen-year-old Sharon, who walks into the classroom near the end of
Jessica's interview, and who "hangs around" with Jessica because there are
so few African American girls in NAI besides her, slowly shakes her head
and swings her feet back and forth as she talks: "My mother makes us use
the bathroom every morning before we goes to school because we doesn't
feel comfortable using that bathroom at school. They still doesn't even have
doors." Jessica and Sharon giggle. Mark, a USC student who assists with
the focus group interviews and also volunteers at a local school, agrees with
Jessica and Sharon: "Those bathrooms are disgusting. I won't use them."
And Sharon points to her photo of Jessica's photo: "Just look at what I use
every day. The floor is awful." "Oh yeah," Jessica adds.

Parents' Response to the Toilet Problem

Several days later, I arrange a meeting with Kim Thomas-Barrios, NAI director, to show Jessica's bathroom photos on PowerPoint slides to a gathering
of one hundred parents who are attending an NAI meeting to discuss their
children's progress in the program. They all become quite animated when
they hear the kids' story about the bathroom conditions. They are express-
ing their opinions by standing up without being called on and offering com-
mentaries about the political culture they feel allows this "horrible condition
to exist," as Cesar's mother puts it. Some parents speak only in Spanish but

speak up anyway with the help of a translator. Maria Lopez, a mother with two children attending NAI, says in Spanish, *"También deberían limpiar el baño* (They should also clean the bathroom)." Another mother adds quickly, *"¿Dónde están nuestros políticos cuando nosotros los necesitamos?* (Where are our politicians when we need them?)"

Tamara Hunt offers what she sees as a solution: "NAI parents should get together and sign a petition or have a town hall meeting. They can also clean the bathrooms and invite the media." The audience responds with loud applause. Luisa Garcia quickly discounts that idea: "We have a lot of problems in this community. We don't need to take on this one. It won't make us look good." The rest of the parents clamor for attention: "It is a coward's response," Maria Lopez says. In fact, the discussion becomes so heated that Dina, a USC student and former NAI student who assists with the interviews and translations, feels compelled to voice her disagreement with the parent. "The school bathroom shows that students do not want to use them because they are filthy and dirty. And we should not allow that to continue. Yes, we should protest." Jake Robertson, Abby's father, agrees:

> My daughter does not like using the bathrooms in school, because they are always filthy and there is no toilet paper and soap. Our politicians in L.A. are not doing anything to make it better for our city and our children. Who do we ask for help? We need numbers to call the city and complain about our needs and our children's needs. No one is listening to the future of our world, which includes our children! I do care and listen to my kids.

Roberta James stands up in the back of the auditorium and speaks before we can call on her. She is not alarmed at Jessica's photos of the toilets: "I work at Manual Arts High School, and I am witness to the condition of the restrooms. I remember as a child I myself did not use the restrooms in school because they were dirty most of the time. We should protest."

The protest does not happen during the two years of this study. Perhaps the protest does not happen because the parents' actions are hindered by the attitudes of some administrators, who strongly believe that the kids are responsible for the conditions of the bathrooms. As Evelyn Morgan, a school administrator who attends a focus group meeting, says, she should get "combat pay for this job. They don't know how to use the bathrooms, having never been told how to use a bathroom."

When I tell Pat Golden, a teacher at one of the local schools, about Evelyn's comments, she agrees with Evelyn. "In our schools the kids trash the bathrooms and break things." She clings to this argument even when I point her to a recent *Los Angeles Times* headline that reads, "District Launches Clean Restroom Hotline." According to Los Angeles Unified School District Chief Operating Officer Howard Miller, conditions at city schools are unacceptable. "Clean, working school restrooms are fundamental," he said.[10]

Should we blame the "ugly" school bathrooms on the kids or on the parents, as Evelyn and Pat imply? Or do we need a deeper analysis of the social causes of these problems? Evelyn seems to support the popular culture-of-poverty assumption that it is the kids' parents who fail to provide traditional family structures for their children. The assumption implies that having the school custodians fix the bathrooms—something Evelyn says they do daily—would not motivate these kids to adopt the values of mainstream culture. As Evelyn suggests, the kids' parents have failed to teach their children proper bathroom etiquette. Evelyn states it as a personal belief based on eyewitness accounts. By blaming the conditions of school facilities on the kids, the adults in this story can sidestep the basic structural problems such as the poor physical conditions and poor quality of most inner-city schools, instead of giving support to these kids.

A major problem with this argument is that it places responsibility for ventilation and rodents on kids, as if they are adults—those who have the power to effect change. Instead, the kids see these adults as avoiding taking responsibility for these social problems.

Evelyn's perspective has a polarizing effect—teachers versus kids, middle class versus poor. And in some cases it may be an issue of racism, but interestingly, many of the teachers in these schools who share Evelyn's thinking are also Latino and Black teachers. A Black teacher uses the phrase "combat pay," as I mentioned previously. And the photos of some teachers in later chapters are Black and Latino. And of course, there are Bill Cosby's comments about knuckleheads. This culture-of-poverty argument allows those like Evelyn and Cosby to ignore the insidious use of "social equality" as an integral feature of correctness and "success."

Maria Garcia, a psychologist who takes part in a focus group of teachers and who has studied the impact of poverty on the development of children's attitudes toward themselves and others, also sees the toilet photos, hears the administrators' comments, and offers another perceptive: "If these kids are destroying the bathrooms, that wouldn't be unusual. They will do this because they are angry about what's going on in their lives."

The ACLU complaint mentioned previously concludes that these conditions expose children to unsafe and unsanitary conditions and could limit their ability to learn in that kind of problematic environment. Moreover, these unhealthy conditions can cause them to disrespect themselves and others like them.[11] Jonathan Kozol would agree with the ACLU findings on the ways in which these conditions affect children's ability to learn:

> No matter how many tawdry details like these I've read in legal briefs or depositions through the years, I'm always shocked again to learn how often these unsanitary physical conditions are permitted to continue in the schools that serve our poorest students—even after they have been vividly described in the media. But hearing of these conditions in [a student's] words was even more unsettling, in part because this student seemed so fragile and because the need even to speak these indignities in front of me and all the other students were an additional indignity.[12]

As one report notes, "Students of color and those living in poverty are far more likely to endure these shocking conditions." It concludes that forcing students to attend decaying schools tells them that they are not valued. These poor conditions can lead to anger, shame, and indifference and promote fighting between students.[13] Mitchell Landsberg, who has studied depression in adolescents, finds in his survey of six thousand South Los Angeles high school students that more than half are frightened by violence in school. One student, who helped organize the survey, summed up the attitude of the students in general: "They see that their school is failing them, their teachers are failing them, there's racial tension and gang violence, and also many feel that their schools are not schools—their schools look more like prisons." A lot of students were depressed because of the conditions in their school and were exhibiting symptoms of clinical depression.[14] I see this in J.D.'s demeanor. He certainly thinks his school and his teachers are failing him, and then there is the racial tension and gang violence. Abby feels the same as J.D., and, as their photos show, all the kids see their schools not as educational institutions but as prisons—both in physical appearance and in the way they are treated by school security guards (more on this later in this chapter). The kids think that they look and feel like prisoners.

Indeed, these photographs of chain links seem to represent a metaphor for the kinds of fences between the lives of these kids—they can see though the chain links but have difficulty climbing over them—and those of the USC students quoted in the introduction.

· · ·

J.D. and many other Willard kids sit in a circle around a large desk as we eat pizza and talk about a number of low self-esteem problems: "We're ignored at school." I have a strong sense that the Willard kids, unlike the lively, feisty, and eager-to-talk NAI kids, are more likely to feel pushed up against that chain-link fence, as in Cesar's picture of his friend Juan (see Figure 5.5). Perhaps that depression I see in J.D.'s, and later in DeWayne's, eyes and voice shows the stress of living in what Harriette McAdoo has called "a mundane extreme environment," racially segregated, economically depressed, and socially isolated.[15] They simply do not have the same support system as NAI kids.

When I drive by two high schools for several weekdays around 3:00 P.M., small groups of students are walking to a bus stop; others are standing at the curbside, waiting for a pickup. Most interesting, I see three police cars parked at the school entrance, the police watching as the students, all wearing white T-shirts, descend the school steps.

The kids certainly do not feel they can trust or even feel secure in their "falling down" school environment. Inner-city low-income kids have little opportunity to have their say about their school environment because they live in households where just handling daily business may take all of their time and energy. The ability to photograph the troubling aspects of their school experiences, along with the sense that they are entitled to something better and that most of their parents support their views, helps shape their perspectives of their school conditions. The truth of the matter is in the photographs. The photos tell a story of poverty, depression, and carelessness. The kids' stories add the insider perspective on what we cannot see—even with our eyes wide open—the feeling of neglect and the hostility they encounter on a daily basis.

A UCLA Institute for Democracy, Education, and Access research report, *Separate and Unequal 50 Years after* Brown: *California's Racial "Opportunity Gap,"* shows that non-White schools are eight times more likely than White schools to have problems with teacher turnover, poor-quality textbooks, vermin, and overcrowding.[16] Piedmont High in Oakland, California, is in an upper-income neighborhood where the parents often contribute as much as $100,000 a year to offset public funds. Those contributions have provided Piedmont with a fully equipped gym, a gleaming basketball court, and sparkling bathrooms. Schools like Piedmont High offer kids a different kind of educational experience. These schools fit Kozol's model of public private schools.[17]

Kozol makes the point about public private schools in his disturbing book *Savage Inequalities*, where he examines the conditions in the nation's schools as well as the personal attitudes and political policies that have created them. Kozol spent two years visiting public and private schools in Chicago, New York, East St. Louis, San Antonio, Washington, and Camden, New Jersey. He saw school buildings flooded with sewage, closets serving as classrooms, classes with no teachers, and buildings where the toilets did not even work. He learned of state school financing formulas that funded affluent districts at a rate fourteen times that of neighboring, low-income districts. He talked with fourth graders studying logic and high school students who could barely read. He was struck by "the remarkable degree of racial segregation" that persisted almost everywhere, which has everything to do with inequality and racial isolation.[18] He also visited public schools in middle-class areas where parents in those neighborhoods would raise "outside" money to buy "certain extras" for the school. As one urban planner told Kozol, "There are boundaries for school districts, but some parents know the way to cross the borders. The poorer and less-educated parents can't."[19]

Kozol argues that once inner-city kids are racially isolated, they get a message: they are to be scorned, shunned, and viewed as contaminated— carriers of plague, almost. The message is clear, especially in schools that are predominantly Black and Hispanic. Kozol found, for example, that "in Los Angeles there is a school that bears the name of Dr. King that is 99 percent black and Hispanic, and another in Milwaukee in which black and Hispanic children also make up 99 percent of the enrollment. There is a high school in Cleveland that is named for Dr. King in which black students make up 97 percent of the student body, and the graduation rate is only 35 percent. In Philadelphia, 98 percent of children at a high school named for Dr. King are black."[20]

My observations support Kozol's argument. I have also visited middle-class schools with twelve to thirteen kids in a class, some who sit in reclining chairs as they debate reading assignments.[21] The students can make use of long rows of sinks and toilets in every bathroom, play musical instruments, and learn Latin. But these are observations of private schools, where the parents have donated as much as $280,000 for a year's upkeep. The race and class structure that supports these school experiences points up the inequities that have developed over time. It is unfortunate that Evelyn, the school administrator, believes parents and kids are at fault for bathroom conditions that have little to do with limited school funds or society's generic, negative perspective of inner-city kids.

6 |

"She's Gettin' Her Learn On"

Through the Eyes of Fourteen-Year-Old Wynette

Wynette, a tall, strikingly pretty African American with light brown eyes, dressed in a white sleeveless blouse and black cut-offs, flips through the twelve photographs she has taken of groups of friends. Wynette sighs before she begins to talk about the photos that she takes. As she puts it, "I took all of these pictures to tell you about the stuff I went through in school." She begins by telling me how she winds up at a number of "terrible schools." Her father, a single dad of two, moves the family quite often before finally settling on Los Angeles, where he has hopes of finding a better-paying job. Because she has had to move so often, Wynette considers herself an expert on the difference between a "good school" and a "bad school," her latest being the "worst." Wynette describes how she feels moving from a suburban school to a crowded inner-city school:

> At thirteen, I moved from one school to another. I went to Washington High School—and that was a big difference. It was way more kids. Like, I'm used to twenty kids in a class and there are like forty kids, forty kids in a math class. They had to squeeze me in the back—so I'm back there with all of these kids, the bad kids, the gang members. They're all bigger than me, and I'm in the back with them. And we didn't have our books, so I had to share with an actual drug dealer.

At this point, Wynette has a deep frown on her face. She continues, "In my class, one kid never did any work. He just copied my paper. And he's getting A's, and the teacher tried to give me a lower grade than him. He copied off of me. It doesn't make any sense." Wynette finds it hard to understand why she always fails her exams:

> The highest grade was a C grade, and I was a straight A student. That was the funny part. I messed up my grade because this teacher wouldn't teach. Instead of being given much needed academic classes, the students were given service class like cooking, and this happens to a lot of students.

She laughs at the irony. "I worked so hard to keep my grades up. I have plans to get a college degree."

According to Wynette, moving from one city to another is not the major barrier to getting a good education. Rather, in her view, the problem has to do with the overworked teachers who have given up on their students and the overcrowded classrooms permeated by a sense of danger.

> And [the class] was so bad because it was so big. So they ran handouts so we had to share tests. I was scared. I mean, we had stuff from the outsiders that would come into our school, from the other schools, and I was really scared. And this drug dealer would always wear a big coat. In August. He also had a joint behind his ear. And nobody ever said [*pauses*] I've seen it. I've seen some people walk right by the teachers. I've seen students sell drugs in class, a big bag of weed.

She adds, without prompting, "And no, he didn't have a hood on. Yeah, he was in the eleventh grade, so I don't know why he was in the ninth grade."

Wynette takes this experience as a lesson in knowing how to survive and maneuver in a dangerous situation by befriending the gang members because "they kind of look out for you."

> One day, I accidentally sat on this bench that was like, I guess it was a gang member's bench. Every day I'd hide out in the ninth-grade center. I didn't know anyone at school. Everyone looked older than me. The teacher said, "We can't hide you in here all the time, so you gotta go."

She begins to cry. She cannot believe that the teacher makes her leave class.

> So I just got my English books and I pulled one out and I'm sitting on this bench and I'm reading. I'm focused. Next thing I know they're talking and he's like, "Nah, nah, let her stay here. She's gettin' her learn on." I'm like, oh my god, these are, like, thugs. And then after that, he would always look after me. He wouldn't let people mess with me.[1]

What disappoints Wynette and the other kids has to do with their perspective of these drug dealers and gang members, some who are not much older than they are, as people who have become victims of the South Central environment. "This world can be an incredibly terrible place for us," she tells me. In her view, the teen drug dealer who sits next to her has to be smart to live in and make money from that kind of environment at such a young age: "You're like a young businessman. You have to learn how to handle business," she says. "They don't know there was no other way for them to deal with this sort of talent they had."

Wynette and I talk about a newspaper article featuring an interview with a popular hip-hop artist, Mary J. Blige, who has taken an active role in talking about her early years living in the inner city. There she became so content with her life that, she says, "I ended up becoming my environment."[2]

> The people hanging around me used me; put my money in their pockets, pushing drugs, alcohol. But it was a far-fetched dream because of all the dream-smashing going on around me. I couldn't even love myself. I ended up becoming my environment. . . . It was bigger than me. I had no self-respect. I hated myself. I thought I was ugly. Alcohol, sex, drugs—I'd do whatever it took to feel better.[3]

Patricia Williams suggests that people who live in what Blige describes as a "dream-smashing environment" can experience a psychological stripping of self in which people will believe in failure. They will learn to believe in stereotypes about their group and may become committed to living in segregated communities.[4] Blige's dream-smashing idea is expressed over and over in Wynette's story of her classroom experiences with gang members who seem to control her school, and of teachers who "didn't teach."

Wynette points to a photograph of a male teacher standing benignly facing the camera, as if to fulfill Wynette's request for a photo (see Figure 6.1).

Figure 6.1

I ask, "What do you mean he didn't teach? Tell me what happens from the beginning from the time you walk into the class." She replies:

> We'd walk into class, and then he would just tell us, "Okay, get your books out and you go to chapter whatever and just read it and, you know, teach yourself." So we would just sit there, and he would sit there in his desk, and he would do his own work, and we would try to read. We played games, made up games, Jerry Springer. Yeah, be talking or writing notes to each other. So that's how we would spend the class time—the whole hour.

Wynette and the other students complain to the NAI staff, but whenever someone from the administration checks the classroom, the teacher picks up a book and begins writing on the board. According to Wynette, "He would tell them that he was doing his job."

Through the Eyes of Fifteen-Year-Old DeWayne

DeWayne sits at the Willard after-school center's corner desk stuffing slices of pizza with mozzarella cheese and salami into his mouth. "I'm hungry," he offers. According to DeWayne, his mother does not have the time to make his lunch, so he makes it himself or relies on the Willard staff to feed him. He spends his after-school hours at the center. He became involved with the center by accident. One day, several months before our interview, DeWayne recalls, his mother, who had to stay at work later than usual, asked him to take his sister to the center, a two-story, gray building located around the corner from a McDonald's and a Domino's pizza place (a location that greatly pleases the center's staff and students).

DeWayne stays at the center to watch his sister receive help with her homework, play a video game, and eat a slice of pizza, given to her by the staff. DeWayne is really impressed with the overall camaraderie between the kids and staff. He begins coming to the center almost every day. DeWayne (along with other Willard kids) says, "It gives me someplace to go after school. It feels good to be here."

DeWayne, who wants to pursue a modeling career, has dyed his short hair a bright red that calls attention to his round face and dark skin. He has been relying on his mother to help him find an agent. But so far, she has refused to help him. "I can't count on her," he says. And so, after he finishes his classes at school, he takes the Blue bus down to the Hollywood area and tries to meet with agents on his own. So, far, he has had no success.

He only wants to talk about his new school, Washington Prep High, and its notorious reputation. Shortly after DeWayne's arrival at the school, a newspaper article publishes a report on the numerous problems at the school. The article, "School Called 'Out of Control': Teachers and Students at Washington Prep High Describe Crime, Sex Acts, Drug Use on Campus," reports that at the school, students are regularly beaten and robbed, they have sex and use drugs in corridors, and pleas for discipline go unheeded by the administration.[5]

According to DeWayne, Washington Prep High is a far cry from the highly regarded Alexander Hamilton High School Music Academy on the edge of Beverly Hills, which he had attended until he was suspended after

Figure 6.2

getting into a fight with a known gang member who lives in the area. It is easy to understand DeWayne's deep disappointment—or perhaps anger. After all, he has had to leave an award-winning music school program that gives students the opportunity to perform at various music concerts and festivals, most notably the legendary Monterey Jazz Festival.

He is so angry at having to attend Washington High that he uses all of his twenty-five photo shots taking photos of his classroom, his teachers, and even one of his friends role-playing a student at his school stealing money from other students.

In that photo, a teenage girl with a large bag slung over her shoulder appears to be sticking her hands into the bag (see Figure 6.2). DeWayne has asked his friend Tanana to reenact to what he says is "a terrible problem of students stealing other students' wallets or other property." He explains, "That's how my friend played it. She is showing how people come along and as soon as you put something down on a bench or chair, they grab it, just like she's doing, and shove it into their bags. People steal everything."

DeWayne points to several photos he took of the back of a classroom being taught by a teacher. The first photo shows a group of students sitting around desks in a classroom (see Figure 6.3). "Why did you take this photo?"

Figure 6.3

I ask. DeWayne responds, "Look at this! The teacher isn't teaching us any-thing at this dumb school. We're sitting around listening to our iPods or looking at movies. You know what he told me? That if I just come to class, I could pass the course."

In the next photo, a rather stout woman stands in front of a school build-ing next to an alleyway (see Figure 6.4). DeWayne explains:

> Look at that. She's our P.E. teacher. And she's supposed to run with us. How can she do that? These people don't care. And see the path next to her? I took the picture also because that's where all the drugs and sex stuff happens at night when no one is around. The teachers try to pretend that they don't know what goes on in that alley. But we all know.

He wants to use the photo of the P.E. teacher to show that the adminis-tration does not care for kids like him: Why else assign "someone who is not in good shape to my P.E. class? That wouldn't happen at Hamilton."

DeWayne claims that the school authorities have not been able to con-trol the drugs, fighting, and other problems that occur at the school.

Figure 6.4

Fighting at School: DeWayne and Nace

DeWayne and Nace (a Willard classmate) do not feel safe at school and try to stay away from getting involved in fights—but to no avail. DeWayne has to fight to show that he is not afraid of the gang member. He cannot back away. According to the code of the inner-city street, he stands the chance of being branded a "bitch-ass nigga" and picked on by other gang members and his schoolmates. According to twelve-year-old Nace, "It's hard not to fight when your homie is being hit." Nace, who giggles every so often and describes himself as a "Mexican that is built like a football player" (something he hopes to become), has to prove his loyalty to his homies. In this world, homies are friends he can depend on to, as he puts it, "watch my back." Most of the kids use the term *homie* to describe members of their peer group who offer support and protection when there is no one else to turn to. I ask, "Anything else you would like to say about your school?" DeWayne says:

> At [Jefferson], there are constantly fights against Black and Latino people, so I don't know why they don't stop that, like, a lot and just expel the kids that fight. I think the school doesn't want to do it and wants to help the children out, but they're just not getting it because

the kids constantly fight, and they just don't want to expel the kids because that might ruin their future.

Like Washington Prep High, Jefferson High School has earned national attention for brawls and fights.[6] The fighting appears to be related to issues larger than simply adolescent angst; the news media have focused a great deal of attention on tension between Blacks and Latinos. According to one article, "Recent, large fights between black and Latino students in Southern California highlight the changing racial dynamics and agendas in the nation." The article states that more than one hundred brawling Black and Latino students have exposed "the enduring myth of Black-Brown solidarity." "In truth," the article goes on to state, "tensions between Latino and black students have always lurked dangerously close to the surface, fueled by the changing ethnic realities in Los Angeles, and America, in the past decade."[7]

Nace remembers his parents talking about two brawls at Jefferson High School that the newspapers claim may have been racially motivated. "Everyone talked about it. My mom's friends wanted to take their kids out of the school, but where would they go?" According to the newspaper's account, the fights leave "several students wounded and a campus at least temporarily split by race."[8] In fact, Jefferson High School gains national attention for the brawls and fights that occur during the school day.

According to the article, the fights raise questions about the ability of students to learn in an environment where they do not feel safe. The school's principal tells the *Los Angeles Times* that racial tensions are "coming out of the community, and into the school."[9] Interestingly, the Black and Latino kids I interviewed do not demonstrate any racial tensions. In fact, they seem cognizant of the need for diversity and a need to participate in making changes that reflect diversity. For example, during Barack Obama's 2008 campaign, at least five Latino kids say that they liked the idea of having a Black president. I remember Juan saying to me that he would vote for Obama if he could, because, as he put it, "He'll do something for kids like me." The Jefferson High principal has a different perspective: "Diversity has almost become synonymous with divisiveness here," he explains. "We don't need any more flash points."[10]

The School Security Guards

DeWayne points to the photo of a friend who he says represents a security guard at his school, except "he's Black and older and has a big stomach" (see

Figure 6.5

Figure 6.5). DeWayne laughs. And most important, DeWayne wants me to know, these guards will have the right to restrain people engaged in disorderly conduct—"just like the real police."

DeWayne and Nace have different impressions of the security guards at their schools. The four security guards at DeWayne's school often ask him, he says, "to empty my pockets," or wave a metal detector over him as they search for weapons—a common occurrence for many inner-city students.[11] In an article critical of metal detectors, the writer asks, "How many firearms have been found in eight years of daily metal searches in Los Angeles?" "Not one," admits Wesley Mitchell, a former Los Angeles chief of police.[12] Several kids say that the security guard checks at the front door make them feel like criminals: DeWayne points out, "I'm not a criminal and I don't deserve to be treated as one." Nace also believes "they aren't really necessary. Most times, you see them walking down the hall talking all the time. Once, they stopped me and took my phone." He laughs. "What are they for anyway, besides taking our phones and kicking us out of the building?"

John Devine's ethnographic study explores the environments in inner-city schools that contribute to the alienation of students like DeWayne. According to Devine, "When most people—Americans or foreigners, even those who live in economically impoverished lands—think about schools, they ordinarily do not think of uniformed security guards, high-tech devices for weapons searches, or the use of police tactics for corridor surveillance." He goes on to say that "students attending New York City's most troubled high schools do so automatically."[13] A similar scenario plays out in DeWayne's and Nace's school security guard stories. For Devine, "Inner-city school corridor life, with its squads of guards, high-tech equipment, and recurring incidents of violence, stands as a stumbling block to those who would restore any vestige of a demythologized humanist tradition" and further alienates students.[14]

In effect, the teachers seem to have given over some of their responsibilities as competent and dependable adults to security guards and metal detectors, thereby preventing them from forming healthy relationships with students like DeWayne and Nace, who take the presence of security guards as one more sign that people like them cannot be trusted.

The teachers' inability to connect with these kids creates the image of teachers as true "outsiders" and thus strengthens the stereotype of students like DeWayne as unmotivated, misbehaving, unteachable inner-city toughs. One poster in an Internet forum, a former schoolteacher, uses his observations about his students to support the theory that inner-city kids are unteachable, a perspective in line with the popular but ill-informed culture-of-poverty theory:

> The students had no respect for me or themselves. They would fight each other and spit at me[,] being totally wild. [E]ven when the dean came in the students gave him no respect. What can we do about getting our children to learn[?] Obviously the parents don't care or these problems would go away. Geeze . . . they ripped up their history books and threw them at each other. How can one person control schools this out of control[?][15]

Is this viewpoint accurate—that these kids and their parents simply do not care about learning? Of course, some kids do have behavioral problems and drop out of school. According to one report, John C. Fremont High School has an official dropout rate of 9 percent. However, it has more than 1,900 students entering as freshmen and fewer than 500 enrolled as seniors, so, as one critic of the report notes, "unless almost 70% of the entering class transferred out and no one transferred in, this school loses more than 9% of its students to dropout."[16] The former teacher quoted above, whose own school experiences may contradict those of the kids in my study, may have had a difficult time understanding why some inner-city kids drop out of school.[17]

Are DeWayne, Nace, and Wynette unmotivated and taking it out on their classrooms, as the poster believes? Jay MacLeod writes about teachers like this: "The equality-of-opportunity line of reasoning may have worked for the middle-class high schools from which most teachers hail, but its utility in an urban school serving low-income neighborhoods is diminished greatly."[18]

Are there alternative explanations for the behavior and high dropout rates of these students? MacLeod argues that it is a myth that any child can grow up to be president. He suggests that the popular idea that "the American Dream is held out as a genuine prospect for anyone with the drive to achieve it," regardless of race and class, is false and misleading.[19]

Wynette, De Wayne, and Nace do not see an open and fair school system full of opportunities for them to progress, as the writer of the Internet post seems to claim. And the high dropout rates hover over these kids like a specter waiting to spirit them away. Still, those rates have been useful to teachers like the writer of the post in supporting the "unmotivated and unteachable" stereotype.

The Teachers through the Eyes of Twelve-Year-Olds
Cesar and Juan

I ask, "What do you think needs to change in your school?" Cesar replies, "Better teachers that actually care. They'll just go into class and they'll just sit there, and they'll take out a book. They walk up and down the halls; they're sleeping, not even paying attention." At the school Cesar attends, only 22 percent of students passed the state exam in English and math in 2007. His school has a reputation for having a high dropout rate and for being among the most violent in Los Angeles.

But Cesar and the others who talk about their photos do not have an understanding of their schools' economic woes. What they see and try to reveal with the help of their five-dollar disposable cameras are the tortured relationships between students and teachers who, perhaps so overwhelmed by their schools' financial problems, do the best they can under the circumstances. Studies find that within five years of teaching, many new teachers leave not only these schools but the profession as well.[20] Older teachers may rely heavily on substitutes to teach classes.[21]

Cesar, who sits across the table from his "best friend," Juan, a skinny middle schooler with a pimpled face, talks about his photos first. In Cesar's photos, the teachers stand at the blackboard or sit at their desks. Some face the camera, intense eyes staring straight ahead. One stands in front of the class, a deep frown on his face. When I first see the photo, before I show it to Cesar, I think that this photo is of his favorite teacher—one who seems to be a dedicated teacher in the middle of instructing his class.

EK: Why did you take this photo of your teacher? [See Figure 6.6.]
CESAR: 'Cause I like some, but I don't like this one. The teacher I most do not like is Mr. Black. Because when he grades you, he eats a burrito and spits on your paper.
JUAN: He was trying to show [his teacher] this camera, [*pauses*] and then he [the teacher] was like, "Yes, you can take it but only without my burrito."
CESAR: I was like, "I need your burrito in my camera," and he was like, "No, you lost your chance." I was like, "I did not lose my chance; I can take it right now." I was like, "I need this for a project, Mr. Black," and he was like, "No! Have you lost your mind?"

Everyone laughs. Juan is also intent on making his point about a teacher he dislikes:

He would be at his desk, and he would tell Rita [about her paperwork], "You missed a period here." He would throw it at her. There was nothing anyone could do. Because he was *Mr. Walker* [*speaking slowly and loudly to emphasize his teacher's authority*].

Both Juan and Cesar have a well-developed sense of fair play and use it to show their appreciation for some of the problems faced by the teachers and the school in general, especially when dealing with problem students. Juan admits that his classmates can be quite a handful for teachers: "The bell rings—like, in my class he keeps us in after the bell rings a long time. Like on Friday he kept us in until almost 3:30 P.M. for talking and interrupting his class." Not all the teachers are like Mr. Black, Cesar and Juan point out. "Mr. Jobs is nice. He was the one who got me into NAI," Cesar says. Juan chimes in, "And I like my history teacher. He's fun."

Still, from the perspective of these adolescents, the teachers are much more of a problem than the kids in the class. According to Juan, "He [the teacher] talks on his cell phone during class."

All the kids are troubled by what they perceive to be teachers who do not care about them, perhaps reinforcing their sense of worthlessness. It is difficult, the kids say, to follow teachers' orders "when you feel the teacher does

Figure 6.6

not see you as a full human being." While a number of reports indicate that the Los Angeles public school system is in deep financial trouble, teachers, who often contend with overcrowded classrooms and students who misbehave, are seen as having failed their students.[22] But Cesar may be too young to understand this problem.

Cesar is disturbed by what he characterizes as an uninformed teacher: "I have a music teacher, and he is not mean. He doesn't know music. I've been like four weeks already, and he has only quizzed us on the same person. This person called Bock [Bach] or something like that." We all laugh. But it says a great deal about Cesar's school's curriculum. It means to him that Latino musicians are not worthy of being taught. Perhaps the curriculum could include works by composer Heitor Villa-Lobos, who is considered the most celebrated Brazilian composer of all time and was a student of Bach's work.[23] Still, Cesar is lucky to have a music class since so many of these classes have been cut in recent years. Two thirds of the kids say they want their schools to offer more ethnic studies classes.

．　．　．

What is the alternative view of these kids' school experiences? As mentioned in Chapter 4, Michael Schwalbe argues that the game is rigged for some.

Schwalbe goes on to say that the kids playing in the game are, by accident of birth, not equipped with the kind of resources and support that can help them do well in school.[24]

According to Melissa Milkie and Catharine Warner's study, children in negative environments—such as classrooms with fewer material resources and whose teachers receive less respect from colleagues—have more learning, externalizing, interpersonal skills, and internalizing problems.[25] To make matters worse, recently another study found that Blacks students are now over three times more likely than Whites to be suspended. While the average suspension rate was 11.2 percent in 2006 in the middle schools surveyed, disaggregating the data by race and gender reveals great disparities in the use of out-of-school suspension. For example, for middle school Blacks, 28.3 percent of males and 18 percent of females were suspended.[26]

According to Milkie and Warner, there are two ways to understand how children's socioeconomic status and race connect to school environments in influencing mental health. First, schools may be a mechanism by which children's status is linked to problem behavior. For example, children attending lower-quality schools characterized by insufficient resources or low teacher morale—often lower socioeconomic status or minority children—may be more likely to act out, have trouble with peers, or feel more anxious than children who enjoy better school conditions—typically children of high socioeconomic status and White children. Second, the issue of whether lower-quality learning environments create more difficulties for those already in a disadvantaged position needs to be examined. In other words, harsh classroom environments may exacerbate the mental health challenges that poor and minority children experience as a result of their socioeconomic or racial status.[27]

Interviews with Three NAI Student Volunteers

In an attempt to gain more insight into these kids' school experiences, I asked six USC students who volunteer at the local schools to give me their impressions of the teachers at the schools. Greg, Taylor, and Bobbi, three USC students who tutor NAI students at the local schools, talk about their volunteer experiences. They all say that they came away from that experience with the impression that the teachers they assist in the classrooms are not interested in teaching these students. For example, one of the teachers asks Greg to take over the class because she has work to do. A teacher asks Taylor to explain to her what six divided by zero equals because she has forgotten.

During the first week of Bobbi's assignment, a substitute teacher reads a newspaper during class. Bobbi also reports that within a three-month period, three different substitutes have taken over a class she tutors. Bobbi and Taylor also say that they do work with a number of exceptional teachers at these schools, but most complain to Greg and the others that they feel overworked. Another teacher admits to Greg that she is thinking about using substitute teachers in her class as a way to get away from the stress of teaching her classes. Greg reports that during a three-week period, three substitute teachers replaced the regular teachers in classes he tutors.

I receive e-mail reports from three other NAI volunteers, Kathy, Max, and Jason. Kathy's e-mail explains:

> I volunteer at Manual Arts High School with NAI and on the first day my mini teams came to the class, one of the teachers we were working with made sure to tell us that ¾ of the students participated in NAI and that we were lucky to have this class to work with and not his other class, his "bad" class. From this experience I believe that teachers interact with NAI students differently than with their peers. I think these kids have low self-efficacy because they are not receiving support from their teachers because the teachers make negative assumptions about them. I think that the NAI students see their teachers interact with their non-NAI peers in a less favorable way and that makes them feel undeserving as well because of so many similarities between themselves and those other students.[28]

According to Max's e-mail:

> In the first three weeks of the assignment, the class had a substitute teacher twice. The substitute teacher did not teach much as he sat at his desk reading a newspaper, while the students were allowed to do anything they want. In one instance, the students were told to watch a movie in class because the teacher had some work of her own to do. At this site, I came away with the impression that the teachers did not care.[29]

And Jason reports:

> Unquestionably, the teaching environment at NAI is nothing like the type of education I received. Looking around the room, it is

evident that these students do not have the same luxuries as I was fortunate enough to have. On the first day of class, the teacher asked the students how many of them had an outside reading book and their dictionary. Only a few had both, of any at all. From my perspective, the reason for this is because their families could be struggling financially and/or their families and they simply do not care. It is really sad.

When the teacher teaches, he does tend to snap at the students—and honestly, quite a bit. I am a strong believer of constructive criticism, and for these students especially, I feel that is the best way to go. In my opinion, the instructor should be doing more of the latter in his lectures. For his classes, I have graded several tests. The last test I graded was on a short story, and the highest grade was a 75%. Over half the class scored a 50% or lower. It was heartbreaking to see, and after giving them back to the teacher, he did not seem the least bit surprised as I was. The test looked basic; very simple reading comprehension questions were asked. These students need hope, and someone to personally motivate them. Sadly, it does not appear that they are receiving that at home, not in the classroom. Three weeks ago, the teacher had to leave his Friday class early for a doctor's appointment. I, along with another student teacher, we're asked to take over the class discussion on the reading. He did not ask much of us, besides read and elaborate on the respective text, yet I felt awkward because I am just a college student. I have no problem performing this task, but in no way am I an authoritative presence to be conducting learning in a classroom. This is a huge flaw that needs to be addressed, because when I am leading the classroom, I not my assistant possess the skills to give these students what they really need. I consider myself very intelligent, yet that is no substitute for an actual licensed teacher.[30]

. . .

Before I ended the interview portion of this study with the kids, five of the thirty-nine NAI students had dropped out of the study, some because they could not keep up with the schoolwork because of other demands and some because they felt trapped in what MacLeod calls "a position of inherited poverty."[31]

What comes through loud and clear in the kids' interviews is a pervasive sense of poverty, despair, hopelessness, and invisibility. Perhaps that sense of worthlessness drives them to find an image, any image, as a stand-in for the real experience. Some, like Wynette, are able to cope with these problems, while others, like DeWayne, lose their motivation and give in to the kind of rage that encourages violence.[32]

Joanne Gray, a recently retired teacher who taught at a local inner-city school with a 95 percent Latino population, shares her observations with me:

> I do think that class, race, and ethnicity play a role in how students behave toward authorities and others. I see children mirror their families' views and know that there seems to be a hierarchy—in other words, Salvadorians are better than Mexicans, the slanted eyes of Asians are mimicked, and derogatory language is used toward African Americans. So yes, there are many undercurrents of racial and ethnic prejudice at my school.

These kinds of unorganized environments with security checks and constant fighting can lead to depression for adolescents like DeWayne, who often seems distant and depressed, especially over having to leave Hamilton High. Nace also seems sad and appears to have little energy. In Joanne Gray's view:

> My overall impression is that they are in many ways like children—active, inquisitive, fun-loving, and enthusiastic. One thing that stands out is how few cultural experiences these kids have had; although most come from loving homes, they seem to spend a lot of time watching TV, playing video games, and going shopping. Also, a lot of the boys in particular have very poor social skills in terms of settling disputes. On the yard, there is a lot of name calling, verbal abuse, fighting, and power struggles. For example, I've noticed that when we play team sports such as kick ball, everyone wants to have the ball, and they don't work together to win. Most are quite poor, and when I bring something to share, they have a hard time [sharing] and beg for more.

Joanne Gray sums up her feelings about her students: "I think it's imperative for all in education to give a school a sense of community and to make children feel they are a voice in that community and that they are vital to it." Wynette, DeWayne, and Nace certainly do not feel vital to their school community.

· · ·

Another way to see these problems is to understand how feelings of worthlessness can hamper some students' academic experience. It can prevent them from having the kind of education that teaches mutual respect and where they can trust in and feel safe in their school environment. Economists Samuel Bowles and Herbert Gintis suggest that the real blame for these social problems lies in a system that lets impoverished and uneducated students become impoverished and uneducated adults. Bowles and Gintis argue that inner-city schools are inherently racist and classist in both content and technique.[33]

Furthermore, the authors suggest that minorities are educated in segregated schools by insensitive teachers and take classes in dilapidated buildings in overcrowded classrooms with irrelevant curricula. Under those conditions, students develop a sense of powerlessness, a disregard of teachers, and a feeling that something better is not for them, leading to doubts about their ability to succeed in life. As a result, they learn to denigrate education, perhaps, as John Ogbu claims, by developing an oppositional culture stance,[34] although the kids in this study do not exhibit that attitude.

Both Ogbu and John McWhorter have only a piece of the puzzle as to why many Black kids do not make it out of the ghetto. Ogbu does not develop the degree to which institutional racism assaults the very fiber of those who live under it, despite the desire to achieve a better education, something the kids frequently mention as a goal throughout this book. McWhorter misunderstands the dynamic of living in a culture based strongly on the individualist ideology—something he seems to strongly believe in.[35] Neither author makes it as clear as the kids in this study do that it seems to matter only to some family members and the USC/NAI tutoring staff whether they succeed or fail. No one offers them the kind of emotionally caring support they need.

· · ·

Jonathan Kozol reminds us that many Americans (for example, the former teacher quoted previously) who live far from our major cities and who have no firsthand knowledge of the realities to be found in urban public schools seem to have the vague and general impression that issues of racial isolation that were matters of grave national significance some thirty-five or forty-five years ago have gradually but steadily diminished in more recent years. The truth, unhappily, is that the trend, for well over a decade now, has been precisely the reverse. Schools that were already deeply segregated twenty-five or thirty years ago are no less segregated now, while thousands of other schools around the country have since been rapidly resegregating.[36]

Perhaps the kids' behavior, as witnessed by the former teacher and blogger mentioned previously and others, is the students' way of making themselves heard above the din of a noisy and uncaring school environment. Or perhaps they fight, as DeWayne and Nace do, as a way of dealing with strong feelings of inadequacy because they cannot fight the school system. Perhaps they use that behavior or, as Blige puts it, "become the environment" as a way to push against forces they do not understand or to compensate for being crowded in by their schools, homes, and neighborhoods. People tend to look at the group that lives close to them to blame—their neighbors or peers, for example. It is much harder to blame those not in your view.

Joanne Gray believes these behavioral problems begin at an early age when these students do not receive the necessary kind of support for academic advancement:

> As early as the first grade, [I can see that the belief] that they are failures starts to set in. By the third grade, I've noticed that many of them are just totally confused. They reach high school; they are expected to begin at the same place as middle-class students—their earlier experiences do not give them the kind of resource needed to do so. So they don't remain interested. Would you?

IV

Kids' Neighborhood Stories

7 |

"I Was Just Scared"

We are often told that minority adolescents are a threat to an orderly society. We focus on their poor academic performance, sexual behavior, drug habits, or gang involvement, yet we fail to examine the ways they feel threatened by society. We also fail to examine the ways in which kids may be active participants in their own lives. According to Margaret Beale Spencer, inner-city adolescents grow up in an environment that is especially precarious and confusing. She argues that in this kind of environment, "instances of resilience-success and competence displayed by vulnerable minority youth in spite of adverse living conditions often go unrecognized, thus denying individuals a sense of success and accomplishment."[1] However, the kids in this study do not drop out or back away; they use their photos to expose a precarious and confusing environment, one that threatens them physically and psychologically on a daily basis, injuring their sense of self-worth.

Roberto, Andrea, and Thomas: Cars, Cars, and More Cars

Roberto, Andrea, and Thomas sit around a small table in a vacant classroom near the NAI office teasing one another about their photos: "Why did you take that one? Ugh." Everyone dresses in some version of the current teen fashion: jeans, white T-shirts, and short jean jackets. No one wears baggy pants or revealing blouses, in accordance with NAI's rules. Twelve-year-old Roberto, who has been involved in the NAI program since elementary school, lives on a street that is "not so bad," as he puts it. "I am saying it's not so bad because we have some nice cars here but [not on] no other streets. But you can't see them over here because we don't do that to our cars."

Twelve-year-old Andrea takes a peek at her cell phone while Roberto begins to spread out photos of his home, his school, and cars. The three kids took twenty-two photos of cars parked in driveways, on the street, and stopped in traffic.

Cars are important to the kids. Roberto's family drives him to school, to NAI meetings, and anywhere else he needs to go. Since Roberto's parents also have to use the car to drive to work, they depend on a neighbor or family members to pick him up after school. A few families do have a second car, but they generally need repair or are on loan to a family member. Andrea's family also has a second car. Her mother bought it from "some kind of website. My dad was really mad. He told her that she didn't know what she was doing." Within a month, the car "just stopped on the street." Now Andrea's mother has to drive her to school, and her father, who works an evening shift, has to pick her up from school and take her to NAI meetings. "Sometimes me and my dad go to Smart and Final and to the mall," a forty-minute round trip down Fiftieth Street and Broadway. The only grocery store in Andrea's area "don't carry anything I want." Andrea looks a little distressed, as if recalling something she cannot buy.

There are few car trips out of South Central neighborhoods for most of the kids. Thomas recalls that once a month (it may have been twice a month; he is not sure), his mother drives him to see his "Auntie Janie." But the visit is short. The family needs to get the car back to his father. Roberto also remembers that his parents take occasional weekend trips to Las Vegas. The family car looks like the one in his photo (see Figure 7.1). He says, "My dad had a Nissan with a body pickup in the back, with a bed cover. The window on my side was broken out, and it had, my dad would always say, three hundred thousand miles on it. And we drove that thing. People were always talking about it."

Thomas laughs. He finds it funny that people talk about Roberto's dad's car. "Those people don't have any car." According to Roberto, his family has a second car, which gives him status among his friends. It does not really matter that the family's second car's tires are slashed after the family leaves it parked in front of a relative's house. His dad is planning to pay for repairs as soon as he finds a part-time job.

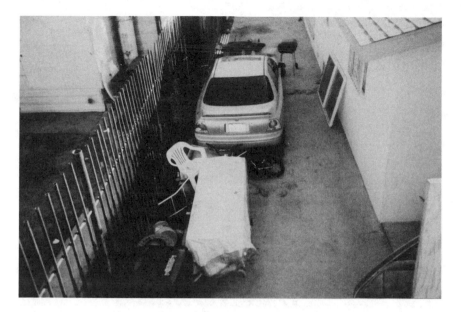

Figure 7.1

Adson and DeWayne

Adson, an African American classmate of DeWayne's at the Willard Center who wears his hair in long braids cascading down his shoulders, has taken photos of cars also. DeWayne and Adson meet with me separately at the Willard Center's office to talk about their photos. DeWayne is proud of his photos, especially the one of his friend's relatives. He took the photo to make a statement about "people who have good relatives who would not buy a car they can't afford." He pauses and adds, "But my relatives buy them anyway. They're so phony. I have an aunt, and she has something like that car." (See Figure 7.2.)

His aunt, who lives around the corner from him in a "tiny" one-bedroom apartment, should not buy such a luxury car, especially in a "neighborhood like mine, where the dogs bark all night long."

In that kind of neighborhood, DeWayne believes, barking dogs mean "trouble. All kinds of people are walking around late at night." He recounts several stories of car tire slashing and car break-ins. But really, he admits, he is upset that his aunt's high-priced car carries higher status and is therefore so much more significant in her life than he is. "She thinks the car makes her better than me." He could use the money she spends on the car for food or maybe just some help with his school expenses. DeWayne takes another

Figure 7.2

look at the photo of his friend's relatives and says, "No. These people were looking like what a couple should look like. They don't wear all those ghetto clothes. And I bet they don't drive those stupid fancy cars they can't afford." (See Figure 7.3.)

I suspect that DeWayne is trying to show me that he has found a couple that represents the order and stability that are missing in his own life. Adson and DeWayne are the same age and attend the same Willard after-school center. But Adson's photos and car stories present a vastly different view of his life, which may explain why his photos paint a brighter side of his neighborhood. He likes his school and is earning B's in most subjects. His father manages a janitorial service. His mother works part-time at the Willard Center so he can see her every afternoon. In Adson's photos, all of the cars are in good condition and nicely parked in front of two-story homes on a tree-lined street. "See, we live in a nice place. It's not like those other places around here."

The Wrecked Cars Stories

In one photo, Adson captures a group of cars against a background of stores and buildings (see Figure 7.4). In fact, according to a professional photographer

Figure 7.3

Figure 7.4

who examines the photo, it shows his potential as a photographer. If only Adson could take photography courses. We both know that, given his parents' income and the distance he would have to climb out of South Central to enter that kind of profession, it is unlikely that he will consider it.[2]

More than half of the kids take photos of cars that need some kind of repair. These kids' car photos, along with their car stories, capture the tremendous instability and disorder they live with on a daily basis. In one of Roberto's photos, two cars are parked next to one another with their hoods up; perhaps both are in the process of being repaired (see Figure 7.5). In another photo, a car with a smashed front passenger side is jammed in front of another car (see Figure 7.6).

Most of these wrecked cars appear to have been involved in some kind of accident. Yet car accidents are not part of the kids' story. Interestingly, parents, teachers, and the college students who see these photos do not mention that wrecked cars may represent a preponderance of car accidents in that community. Instead, a few say that these photos fit the general stereotype of the poor. As Theresa, the USC student I quote in Chapter 1, put it, "Damaged cars are typical to see in poorer neighborhoods. They don't have the dollars to fix cars, so it's left there." Certainly, the large number of cars in

Figure 7.5

Figure 7.6

such disrepair is an important sign of poverty. Given that common assumption, and one with some merit, I expect that the kids will answer the "What do you want me to know about this picture?" question with stories of car repair problems.

The kids do talk about poverty but indirectly. After all, they are inner-city kids, and they present their perspectives of a neighborhood far removed from America's mainstream, in which inner-city kids are often described as "hood rats," according to Roberto, Andrea, and Thomas. These car stories are also intermingled with stories of gangs and violence they see or, in some cases, experience.

Roberto, Thomas, Andrea, and Lupe: Stories of Gangs and Violence

EK: Why did you take this picture of a park? [See Figure 7.7.]

ANDREA: I remember when I used to ride a bike around the park. Yeah. I never do that anymore. My mom would, like, always come outside and get me. Gangs come out there in the late afternoon and make a lot of noise. Like AWAWWWA. [*Everyone laughs.*]

Figure 7.7

THOMAS: No. It sounds like this. [*He makes a sound similar to Andrea's, and everyone laughs.*]
EK: So if you don't play outside anymore, where do you play?
ANDREA: I don't.

Thomas interrupts us. He cannot wait to tell his story, which he seems to enjoy. "My mother tells me not to talk to strangers. And to carry a bat in the car," he says. "Your parents have a bat in their car?" I ask.[3] Thomas is so intent on telling his story that he does not see Andrea shuffling around the rest of his photos. He continues:

My mom and my sister and me, we went away to Big Bear. I don't know what that street is called, but it's a really dangerous street. It's, like, with some prostitutes right there at the red light. So when we stopped, this guy came over from one side, and then he was like, "You want some gum?" And we were like, "No." And then this guy came on the other side and got inside our car and drove off with us inside in the back—me, my mom, and my sister. And then my mom got the bat. [*Pauses*] See, it comes in handy. She got the bat and went [*raises his arm as if holding a bat*]. Then the police came, and they said that it was a good idea to have a bat in the car.

Thomas's mother, who was sitting directly behind the carjacker, pulled out a bat lying on the floorboard. "She was going to bash in that guy's head. He jumped out of the car and ran away."

Twelve-year-old Lupe waves her hands and says:

Once, me and my mother were at the laundry, and then all of a sudden, this man comes up and started shooting the whole place, and we had to be backed into cars going fast, and they already crashed my sister's car and my dad's car [*pauses*] and, um, they need to put bumps [on the street] because they are always going really fast.

I ask, "Why did they crash into your sister's car?" Lupe responds:

The lady said that she was picking up something and then that she accidentally bumped into it and then the other lady that crashed my dad's car. So that's happened to me twice with my sister and my dad's car. Our house is like a big parking lot, and the day before, we were going to get a gate because we did not trust the people on that street, and on that day, our car was stolen.

"What did your parents do about it?" I ask. Lupe says, "They called the police, but the police did not come until five hours later." Roberto chimes in, "When they crashed into my mom's car, they also took a long time to come."

To get an alternative perspective of the photos, I ask Megan, Kenny, and others from the group of twenty-one USC students to watch the PowerPoint photo slides. When Megan hears about Lupe's five-hour wait for the police, she recalls the many times she has attended campus parties where "someone called the police and they always show up right away when we're drunk." Everyone laughs. Kenny suggests that the police respond "more quickly to a party of drunken USC students than they would to a car break-in in a South Central neighborhood because inner-city neighborhoods are considered to be dangerous." In other words, the police will face nothing more dangerous than drunken college students with foul language and bad attitudes, while it is anyone's guess what can happen when dealing with inner-city residents. Perhaps the police, as many outsiders do, interpret car break-ins as an inability of inner-city residents to "clean up their act."

Jason, Jorge, Albin, and Antonio

Thirteen-year-old Jason, an African American, lives on a street inhabited by the notorious Black P Stone Nation. He has taken five photos of late-model cars parked in a front of a grocery store (see Figure 7.8). "This street looks good," he says. Perhaps because it is often difficult to see behind the façade, we all agree. But the reality, according to Jason, who sits at classroom desks next to Antonio, Albin, and Jorge (NAI students), is that at night, when he is just getting to sleep, he hears "loud noises." Twelve-year-old Jorge tells a similar story.

Early one afternoon, I decide to drive down some streets near Jason's neighborhoods. The neighborhood seems ordinary—cars are moving along at moderate speed. People are walking along the streets as they do in any community. Jason lives across the street from a strip mall where small businesses—M&P convenience store, BR Cleaners, McDonald's, Thai Food Express, Mr. Pizza—are packed like sardines into small spaces. A small truck with a "Los Mejores Tamales" sign is parked on the corner of the street. Nothing seems out of the ordinary, although Jason has a different view of his street:

> Well, by the time I was five years old, I was just scared. Like, you hear loud noises. You've seen the movie *Fresh*? Because there's an actual

Figure 7.8

scene that reminded me so much of what happened. It was about this boy who lives in the 'hood, and he learned to play chess from his father. Anyway, in one scene, the people start shooting, and the kids run to the window, and bullets are coming through the window right next to him. When I saw that, it was like that actually happened to me. [*His voice trails off.*]

Jorge has taken a picture of a tree (see Figure 7.9).

EK: Jorge, why did you take the picture of the tree?
JORGE: I like looking at that tree.
EK: Why?
JORGE: 'Cause it's peaceful.
EK: Do you wish you were somewhere else, or does it make you think you were somewhere else?
JORGE: Yeah.
EK: What do you dislike about your neighborhood?
JORGE: The mean guys. [*He begins to stumble over his words.*] They, they, they, they think they are gangsters and stuff. One of the kids that lives around me and he had his hood on and point his little knife at me, and I felt like kicking him right in the crotch. 'Cause he was tryin' to scare me. And he has been in jail before. And [the gangsters] had broken into my house, like, twice. Everybody was in the house. Everybody was asleep. They took our TV and stuff. We woke up just as they got away. That's why my mother wants me to go to USC. To get away.
EK: What about you guys? What do your neighborhoods look like?
ALBIN (*talking over Jorge*): Same thing. It's a ghetto.
ANTONIO: I live by Crenshaw, and there's an alley in the back. And you can hear people screaming, and, like, I can't go to sleep because you can hear people dealing.

According to Jorge, drug dealers use the alley to sell drugs.

JORGE: You could smell it.
EK: How do you know what it smells like? [*Everyone laughs.*]
JORGE: It's really nasty. No, I haven't done that. [*Everyone laughs.*]
ALBIN: They have drive-bys on my block. It was a long time ago. This abandon house this lady owns. But she never goes there,

so these gang members, they went inside the house, and I don't know, but they were doing stuff in there. And then one time, the police came and caught them. And they stopped for a while. But then they went back and burnt down the house. It's, like, right across the street from my house. [See Figure 7.10.]

Jorge fidgets in his chair while Albin finishes his story. He is eager to tell another story. In fact, it becomes a competition among the group as to who can recount a story about gangs. These stories also indicate a deep desire to express fears.

JORGE: There was a shooting in my neighborhood. They shot at this guy. The guy also used to be a gangster, and now he's not anymore. They [the gangs] almost tried to kill his whole family.

EK: And that's in your building.

JORGE: Yeah. I live in a house, not an apartment. And all kinds of people live there.

EK: Well, what do you think of that?

ANTONIO: How are young people supposed to live their life just having bad memories? Right now I'm distant from everyone, except

Figure 7.9

Figure 7.10

the people in NAI. And my mother got robbed, and our house has been robbed seven times. My mother, she just moved back to Arizona. Now I have friends, really good friends. And well, I don't see any more family. My mother visits every month. But I never see my other family. They live in California. But they never visit.[4]

The problem of children of immigrant parents being left behind as parents find work in other cities or states is nothing new. Lisa, a staff member at NAI, reports that the most difficult part of her job has to do with persuading parents to stay in the country so that their children can graduate from the program and apply to college. One interesting example of this kind of situation is a fifteen-year-old who attends every tutoring section. Lisa finds out that her parents moved back to Mexico, leaving her to raise her two ten- and twelve-year-old sisters. She manages to complete her program at NAI and maintain an A average in school. Lisa continues, "But we didn't know of her circumstance until she graduated. This is the kind of thing we try to stay alert to, but sometimes the kids are ashamed of their situation and won't report it. The good news is that she told her parents to come get the kids because she had been accepted in college."

Stories about Graffiti and Tagging Photos

Three kids bring in photos of graffiti and tagged walls. Why do they take those photos? According to fourteen-year-old Marlena, who has taken several photos of a tagged wall, "Well I want to say is—that that picture of the graffiti is on the walls of [a] house? It's like all the buildings with graffiti all over it. I would like to change it." (See Figure 7.11.) "Why does that bother you?" I ask. She says, "Because, like, at school, the teachers see graffiti and tagging on the walls, and they blame me and my friends. We don't tag."

Figure 7.11

Marlena gives me a determined look. Clearly, she sees her tagging story as a way to fight back against the perception people have of people like her. All the kids seem to be using the photos as a strategy to disturb negative stereotypes.

Twelve-Year-Old Angel and Christina

Angel and Christina, both NAI kids, have a great deal to say about graffiti and tagging. Angel may be twelve years old, but she projects a serious and mature demeanor. She dresses in black, a color typically associated with the Goth culture—her jeans, T-shirt, and sweater all black and her jet-black hair hanging to her shoulders. She gives the impression of a Latina with a unique sense of herself. Angel, who is bright and opinionated about anything relating to her neighborhood, has also taken photos of tagged walls.

EK: How would you describe your neighborhood?
ANGEL: Both safe and dangerous.
EK: What do you mean?
ANGEL: There are no gangbanging. They don't tag. So it's calm, and you can barely hear the cars. But I see tagging on the street three blocks away.
EK: What makes tagging dangerous?
ANGEL: Because you know that there is gangbangers around there.

Some people assume that tagging and graffiti were started by inner-city kids or gang members. However, graffiti was started by a short Greek American kid named Demetrius in the late 1960s. He was certainly not the first teenager to think of writing something in permanent ink on someone else's property. But the ubiquity of his neatly written signature—TAKI 183—and an article about him in the *New York Times* contributed to making him into a kind of folk hero, which inspired hundreds of imitators and, by general agreement among urban historians, made him the forefather of the modern graffiti movement.[5]

Christina, who wears brighter colors—a white T-shirt and green shorts—is quiet and thoughtful. There may be a difference in dress and attitude between the two friends, and Christina smiles more often than Angel, but Christina's description of life in South Central matches Angel's. She lives around the corner from Angel on a street she describes as "not really that great." She adds, "And we have a lot of tagging on our street."

ANGEL: Now you hear the story in the papers of the woman who [was] taking her kids tagging. A mother had her kids in the car, and they were tagging; the police arrested them. They first thought it was the kids, but the mother was driving the car, and the kids would jump out of the car and tag. How is tagging a crime? [*Speaking loudly*] *Tagging* is not a crime at all to me. It is just an art. It depends what they tag. If they tag a gang's name, then that is something, but most of the time, it is art inspiration, and this place, me and my mom pass by there once a month or something, and people were all standing around. A gang member died, and I think he was famous, a Crip.

CHRISTINA: The one who wrote the book.

EK: Do you mean Tookie Williams?[6]

ANGEL: Yeah. Some had pictures of Tookie. So now that's art. But what is the other tagging that is not art?

CHRISTINA: The writing that they do on the walls and then other gangs come and cross out the gangs. People confuse tagging with graffiti. Graffiti is art. Tagging involves gangs. [*Pauses*] I know that they killed some guy. Yeah. My neighbor told us the day before that they killed another guy.

EK: So, you've heard that stuff about the gangs—the Black gangs and the Latino gangs?

ANGEL: Yeah. They just shot a little kid and [someone] called the police. She was with her dad.

CHRISTINA: And the police pleaded with people to step forward, and then they got one guy, and then he made a plea and asked people to step forward, and it was someone who knew [the killer], and [the police] were saying that it was very good that someone in the community was stepping up.

ANGEL: Yeah. See, that shows that not all Latinos want to be in gangs and stuff.

Angel is all smiles as she makes this point. She is keen on presenting herself as more knowledgeable about gangs, graffiti, and tagging than the outsider interviewer. Angel takes a breath before she finishes talking about her photos: "Kids live in a dirty environment; their houses are in the middle of trash, graffiti. Seems like the city doesn't care." What is interesting, and a surprise to most of the parents and college students who read their comments on

PowerPoint slides, is the level of confidence the kids have in their assessment of their neighborhoods.

The Broken Window Theory

Bruce H. Rankin and James M. Quane argue that "social isolation, which refers to the lack of contact or of sustained interaction with individuals and institutions that represent mainstream society, is a mechanism that plays a major role in the disadvantaged status of the ghetto poor."[7] These authors suggest that kids, like those in this study, are doubly disadvantaged—by the individual experience of poverty and by the concentrated poverty of the neighborhoods in which they reside.

One way to see the kids' descriptions of wrecked cars and gang problems is to apply the broken window concept, developed by George L. Kelling and James Q. Wilson.[8] The idea was introduced as an approach to combating crime. According to the authors, a community's tolerating loiterers and disorderly minor offenders shows the apathy of the community, just as a small broken house window that does not get mended in a considerable time represents the apathy of the house owner or the absence of people who care. The passersby take the broken window for granted. In time, they even stop taking note of it. But a deep-seated mental note is made that nobody cares. According to this theory, the broken windows act as a signal for petty thieves to steal, for birds to make their nests, for pests to enter, and, in time, for the whole structure to deteriorate. The broken window concept also attempts to establish a link between neighborhood disorder and crime victimization. This concept has been used by several police departments, notably the New York Police Department, as a way to combat crime.

The idea of the broken window is based on principles set forth by sociologist Émile Durkheim, who argues that social control in a society is affected by the collective conscience and shared belief systems of the social organization in question (in this case, the neighborhood). These shared beliefs and common values exist outside the individual within that group, and a collective identity becomes possible because the members of that group share living conditions and similar environmental influences.

The broken window concept has not completely proven true. While disorder does lead to the impression of a crime-ridden community, no relationship exists between the fears of the residents—in this case, the kids who reside in the area—and the impact of the conditions they see on their sense of self-worth and their sense of safety and security. These kids use the photos to dispute their collective identity.

In this community, the kids and their parents have so little connection with authorities and others—there is such a paucity of relations with the larger community—that they have to do whatever they can to protect themselves. According to these kids, living in a highly segregated and depressed inner city means that they are likely to be victimized by another inner-city resident. Living in the inner city means being exposed to some form of abuse—the threat of violence or, in some cases, the act of violence—almost on a daily basis. Living in the inner city means that they cannot ride their bikes or sleep undisturbed by gunshots or drug users needing a fix.

Shelley E. Taylor, Rena L. Repetti, and Teresa Seeman look at chronic stress, mental distress, coping skills and resources, and health habits and behaviors to explore how unhealthy environments can get "under the skin" to create health disorders. The authors define unhealthy environments as "those that threaten safety, that undermine the creation of social ties, and that are conflicted, abusive, or violent. A healthy environment, in contrast, provides safety, opportunities for social integration, and the ability to predict and/or control aspects of that environment."[9]

In isolated communities like South Central, Thomas's mother carries a bat in the car (and in Chapter 9, Marcus's grandmother carries a gun). Angel has to know the difference between tagging and graffiti—it is, after all, about how to survive a physically unhealthy environment, where all around them they see signs that no one cares. Yet somehow, they manage not to point their fingers at their parents, which is the tendency on the part of many children of this age. Although DeWayne is angry that his mom does not spend more time with him, he does not blame her for the changes in his life.

The kids trust in their own abilities to construct their world in ways that give texture to their lives, as they know them. In their view, the car stories are about the impact of gangs, violence, and discrimination by the police, which, of course, are some of the characteristics of economic inequality. These middle schoolers, who are spending their young lives coping with the consequences of economic disparity, present a more nuanced and deeply disturbing photo of their lives than the culture-of-poverty idea that minority kids are likely to grow up in dysfunctional families that deviate from the norm of mainstream America.

The kids' story of their lives also differs from that provided by John Ogbu's oppositional culture theory.[10] These kids do not, as Ogbu's study finds, portray an antieducational or "acting white" stance, as do the kids in his study. Instead, their ability to use the photos as a way to speak to us offers us greater insight into the cost of living in the inner-city than previous analyses of inner-city kids. Nonetheless, as Herbert Gans reminds us, racial minorities tend to be vulnerable to negative labels that are transformed and magnified into character failings.[11]

The kids sitting before me with photos in hand certainly look small and vulnerable. I am reminded of the characters in Ray Bradbury's novel *Something Wicked This Way Comes*.[12] In that story, two thirteen-year-old boys have a harrowing experience with a nightmarish traveling carnival that comes to their midwestern town. The novel combines elements of fantasy and horror, analyzing the conflicting natures of good and evil and how they come into play between the characters and the carnival. Certainly, Thomas, Angel, and the others as characters in the South Central carnival must deal with the conflicting natures of the good they see from their involvement in NAI and Willard and the violence that leaves them with a sense of horror.

Garbage, Alleyways, and
Painted Doors

Manuel, Danielle, Spencer, and Antonio

One Saturday, after attending NAI's Saturday Academy, where they meet with tutors from 9:00 to 12:00, Manuel, a thirteen-year-old Latino, and Danielle and Spencer, both twelve-year-old African Americans, come bouncing up the stairs to the second-floor USC classroom. They have agreed to share their photos with two other NAI classmates. But first they consume potato chips and cookies and make fun of a popular TV program. Finally, they settle down, although they do look a little bored. I lay out the photos—in all they have taken eighty-one photos (twenty-seven each) of their neighborhoods and friends.

The interviews start slowly, but the kids begin to open up with every passing minute. They talk about some of the photos they took around their neighborhoods. Manuel is the first to feel the most comfortable and enthusiastic about his photos. He tells me that he has taken photos of cars, his home, and other buildings near his home. As soon as he begins to mention his photographs, Danielle and Spencer catch on and begin describing the photos that they have taken. While some photos are of neighborhood streets and homes, there are also photos of their friends gathered on a street.

"Why did you take this picture?" I ask Manuel, referring to a photo of a large mound of trash piled up against a cement barrier on a neighborhood street (see Figure 8.1). He sits up straight in his chair and says, "Look at what

Figure 8.1

we have to put up with. That's what they think of us. The city does not care to clean our area we live in."

Spencer and Danielle look at Manuel's photo. Spencer, who lives three blocks from Manuel, rushes to speak before Manuel can finish his point. Spencer points to a photo he has taken of his tennis shoes pointing at some object (see Figure 8.2). He explains:

> It's a dead squirrel. I just thought it was nasty because they just ran over it, and they left it there for a long time. I decided to take a picture of it to show the USC people how animals could get hurt so quickly. They just don't come to our street. It was there for like maybe three weeks. They never picked it up; it just faded away.

Without explaining whether "they" refers to USC students or city services, Spencer rushes to talk about his sighting of a couple of empty snack bags near his home—as if to emphasize the lack of city services. The significance of the kids' comments becomes clear to me after I attend my second parents' meeting, a week later. But at the time, the photos I see and talk

Figure 8.2

about with the kids seem to have only minor importance when compared with other topics we focus on that day, such as drugs, gang activities, and home robberies.

"Shoot 'em up" and "rob 'em" stories tend to catch everyone's imagination. In the minds of Spencer and Manuel, garbage and dead squirrels are also important because they reinforce the popular but negative dangerous and dirty stereotypes in which neighborhood "ghetto thugs" are biologically and culturally incompetent kids who are unable to adhere to mainstream values of cleanliness.

Spencer and Manuel talk about a blogger who writes about his volunteer job cleaning up inner-city parks: "All the trash [was] on the ground next day and the trash can [was] almost empty. It's ingrained, there's no easy solution."[1] Spencer and Manuel shake their heads. Danielle laughs: "What a stupid person!"

The Alleys and Houses

"Why don't you start by telling me why you took this picture of this building?" I say, referring to a picture Danielle took (see Figure 8.3). Danielle says:

Figure 8.3

I will tell you about my neighborhood. I grew up about ten minutes away from here. Um, I didn't really play in my neighborhood because it wasn't safe. So what I would do would just be to go to my friend's house. And I would, you know, play with them there . . . because my neighborhood wasn't safe. I live next to an alley, so that's not safe for me to be outside.

Spencer points to the building and says, "Yeah! There's some fake sign on it in the back that says 'Welcome.' What kind of sign is that for this dumb building? Drug dealers are in the back."

> EK: What about you guys? What do your neighborhoods look like?
> SPENCER: Same thing. It's ghetto.
> EK: What do you mean it's ghetto?
> SPENCER: Like we have in the back, there is an alley. It looks like this picture. [*Points to Figure 8.4.*]
> DANIELLE: That's where all the crackheads and drug dealers go.
> SPENCER: It's by Crenshaw. There is an alley in the back. And I always hear a lot of people there.

Figure 8.4

EK: So what do you think is going to happen if you go outside your house?

SPENCER: They will jump over the fence. My dad is smart. He puts bar handles so you can't get over.

EK: How do you know there are drug dealers that live behind your house?

SPENCER: You could smell it. You could see it when they are selling it.

EK: So, do you like that? Do you wish you were somewhere else?

Antonio, who arrives in the classroom just as Spencer finishes his sentence, begins nodding his head vigorously. Manuel says, "Yeah. I wish I were somewhere else." Danielle and Spencer nod in agreement. Antonio points to his photo of a pink house badly in need of repair. Spencer says, "Yeah. See that building?" He points again to Figure 8.4, which shows of the back of a supermarket that is also in bad shape.

Perhaps inner-city kids like Manuel develop an internal model of reality to explain and understand the world around them. Manuel may not have liked living with gangs and guns, but "I can handle it," he says. In an ideal world, Manuel can reach out to others for help in understanding and perhaps dealing with the effects of the violence he says was all around them.

The buildings and houses in the photos seem to produce a great deal of anxiety, confusion, anger, and fear in the kids. But in this environment there is little they or their parents can do to change those fears.

I ask, "Anyone else seen anything like that in their neighborhood?" At that moment, thirteen-year-old Alberto, who joined the focus group late, responds and launches into a story about his next-door neighbor:

> Not like that. Just the drugs. The house next to me, there are a lot of trees, and you can't see anything. One day, he [next-door neighbor] offered me some drugs, and I got scared and ran and told my dad. And my dad got mad and told him not to do that again. And that guy listened, but then he offered my sister some, so then [my dad] got mad. The guy was like—every night at 1:30 he would start making noises like a bird. There were signs for everyone to come, and then the cops came, and he had a gun, and then they stopped and left to go and catch him.

We look though other photos. One picture of a pedestrian crossing sign rests on top of the pile (see Figure 8.5). When I see this photo, I am convinced that Spencer took it simply because he was running out of things to photograph and needed to finish off the shots. Why else would he take

Figure 8.5

that photo? Once again, Spencer and the other kids use photos as a way to communicate their feelings about something that otherwise would go unnoticed. Spencer wants to make a point about stop signs but does not have a photo of one, so he uses the photo of the pedestrian crossing sign instead.

EK: Spencer, why did you take a picture of the traffic sign?

SPENCER: You know those stop signs. [*Pauses*] They should put more stop signs because sometimes you can't even see [what's coming]. [*Pauses*] You know, like when you are going straight [*pauses*] and there are some bushes there [on the corner], and you can't see [through] those bushes [*pauses*], and then imagine since they don't have a stop sign, then that is where you crash.

EK: Did that happen to you or your family?

SPENCER: Not me. I'm too young to drive. [*Everyone laughs.*] But, yeah, to my mom.

EK: What are some positive things about your neighborhood?

SPENCER: The street where I live is calm now.

ALBERTO: I like it when there is a [block] party, and they give us food and food from McDonald's. Like, my neighbor has a party; they are like, "Come on over," and they give you a plate with the chicken and the rice and, like, the soda and stuff.

He has had a friend take a photo of a McDonald's bag and refers to it to make his point (see Figure 8.6).

EK: So, you can say you have a friendly neighborhood?

ALBERTO: Yeah, and then when we barely moved in, they bought a basket of fruit and stuff like that and was like, "Welcome to the neighborhood." And we skateboard.

Gang Signs in the Ghetto: Isolation and Alienation

Alberto pulls out a photo of his friend sitting near skateboards, making what appear to be gang signs (see Figure 8.7). Alberto's photo of a friend's gang signs and the photo of the NAI kids also making gang signs raise the question of why kids who choose a path so different from those caught up in the gang culture still need to relate to the gang culture to some degree. As mentioned previously, it may seem culturally relevant to kids in inner-city communities when they feel isolated from other cultures. When kids are restricted to a

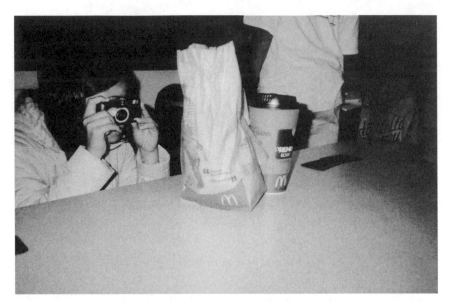

Figure 8.6

Figure 8.7

small space—in the case of these kids, their street or neighborhood no more than ten blocks from USC—they can feel small and squeezed into tiny homes on narrow streets where they stay behind locked doors. Or if they do play outdoors, they are limited to a particular area and to the culture of the gang. I remember Spencer and other kids' comments about living in the "ghetto."

All the kids and parents throughout these interviews refer to their South Central community as a "ghetto" and not the more politically correct term "inner city" that I use. When they use the *ghetto* term, we are describing two different environments. In other words, there is a nuance between the terms *ghetto* and *inner city*. According to the *American Heritage Dictionary*, the inner city is defined as "the usually older, central part of a city, especially when characterized by crowded neighborhoods in which low-income, often minority groups predominate." A ghetto, though, is formed in more distinct ways: "As ports of illegal entry for racial minorities, and immigrant racial minorities."

Spencer's use of the term *ghetto* lends a richer and more deeply textured feel to his experiences than the more academic and cool-sounding term *inner city*. In his story, the ghetto is darker and more dangerous than the lighter, brighter inner city. According to the definition, a ghetto occurs when the majority uses compulsion (typically violence, hostility, or legal barriers) to force minorities into particular areas when economic conditions make it too difficult for minority members to live in nonminority areas and where the minority group actively chooses to segregate itself physically and socially from the majority.

In the case of the kids in this study, they not only are segregated from other communities but are required to segregate themselves from other kids in their own community. Spencer says, "I don't go to the park." Danielle says, "My mom will not let me go anywhere past the street she live on." In fact, the kids live in a modern kind of isolation. On the one hand, and even without a large income, they plug into the latest technology of cell phones, have televisions in every room, and wear the latest fashions, as Wynette points out. "This is some new stuff I just bought." (See Figure 8.8.)

On the other hand, they have limited access to a vision of life outside the "ghetto" other than what they see in the media—for example, one of Spencer's favorite sports: "I see hockey and football on TV mostly. I went to one football game with my uncle. But so far no hockey games."

Spencer and Alberto do not see examples of middle-class people in his community (one reason DeWayne takes a photo of a middle-class couple; see Chapter 7). Since most in their community are in the same socioeconomic situation, the only other culture they see is considered as dysfunctional as

Figure 8.8

their own (for Latinos, it would be the Black culture; for Blacks, it would be the Latino culture).

Their social world is limited to the same areas of the city. In fact, Danielle describes her travels as in a circle: "I go with my mom up to Vons [six miles from her house], and sometimes we go on to Century City [a fifteen-minute drive] if Mom have to buy clothes, [and then we go] back to my house." Interestingly, the trip to Century City gives Danielle a way to observe the social class closely associated with USC students. But still she sees few signs of the middle class in South Central. She may pass USC students jogging past her or spot them in Superior Supermarket or Ralphs. But a few incidents have indicated that unless something drastic happens, these two groups are going to maintain their distance, at least for a while.[2]

Danielle, Spencer, and Manuel live within ten blocks of their school and USC. All of the kids' parents rent their apartments or, as in the case of Kyle and a few others, their houses. Most of the kids describe their community mainly as "dangerous" and a tough place to live. What is important to re-member in considering their analysis of life in this dangerous place is that none of them have traveled far outside their community except for the oc-casional car trip to Las Vegas.

Anselm Strauss suggests that the concept of "orbit" could apply here to say something about space: "the chief efficacy of the term 'orbit' is that it di-rects attention to special movements of members of social worlds."[3] The idea of limited space, Peter Orleans argues, "is especially dangerous if the percep-tions of middle-class analysts are taken as representative of the population at large."[4] Urban life has a reputation as an essentially alienating and disor-ganized venue—chaos. Orleans makes the point that we should continually check our worldview with that of others, especially because our social worlds all too often touch but do not interpenetrate.

The Parents' Meeting

At my second meeting with the parents, I bring up the PowerPoint slide with the kids' photos and comments about the trash and alleyways. One hundred parents, including the parents of Danielle, Spencer, and Manuel, are present at the meeting. The kids' photos and comments lead to a vigorous and some-times heated debate about who should be responsible for the conditions of the street. Almost half of the parents blame themselves for the trash pileup depicted in Manuel's photo. Manuel's father, Paolo, puts it this way: "The responsibility is ours. We are not being good parents. What about our kids? How did we bring them up? We are responsible. We have to put more of this social responsibility on ourselves."

Almost at once, several parents raise their hands to speak. Danielle's father, speaking softly and hesitantly, begins to protest the other parents' views: "I am good parent. My son is good son, and these kids are right." Spencer's father stands up. He is visibly upset when he speaks:

> Yes, yes. He is right. I work in Beverly Hills, and I can see that there are machines cleaning up the alleys and the streets twice a day. The politicians have forgotten about South Central Los Angeles. The political figures do their jobs in Beverly Hills but not in South Central L.A.

Immediately following that comment, a parent waves her hand: "The same happens in Santa Monica, Palos Verdes." A few parents whisper to each other; this issue of where to place responsibility has hit a nerve. Everyone wants to have their say, including this mother, who agrees with Paolo's parental-responsibility perspective but adds a caveat: "Most of us do see the trash on the street, but we don't call to complain. We have to take the initiative to pressure our city to clean it up."

Danielle's mother feels so strongly about this argument that she does not wait to raise her hand: "Yeah, we have to call and complain." That comment leads Paolo to say:

> Just a minute now. Bring your attention to that the economy is very bad. We have to tighten our belts. This is a very, very bad time. We can't keep on demanding. One day we may just die altogether. Our concentration should be what we can do. This is not the time to ask the country for help.

This debate even catches Spencer's mother, Marian, who stands up to have her say. "So, parents have to accept their second-class citizenship? Why not? I bet the Beverly Hills, Hollywood, or Los Feliz parents don't blame their kids, themselves, but blame the city."

A woman sitting directly in front of Marian agrees. She takes the position that aside from the fact that NAI is a great program, it is important for parents to recognize that these kids do not live in an NAI bubble. As she puts it, "They walk on these same streets. We cannot ignore what is happening in our community. Our kids are still part of our community." Marian wants the parents to take a more active stance. Her daughter has e-mailed Mayor Villaraigosa, writing that she was scared to walk in her neighborhood. Marian says, "The kids need to learn to voice their complaints and think that adults will listen. All of us live in the ghetto, but we fail to get involved. People are passive and complain but don't make sure the city does its job."

A number of parents loudly applaud these comments. Others nod in agreement. A few, including Manuel's father, Paolo, who warns them about demanding change because of economic conditions, sit stone faced. The parents are quite willing to voice these views, often emotionally, in a public arena. Others take a proactive approach. These parents certainly contradict the culture-of-poverty notion that they are too permissive in raising their children and that children raised in inner-city environments have a different orientation to life when compared to middle-class children. I suppose one can argue that these NAI parents are of a special breed and therefore do not fit the general population of inner-city parents. But it is worth noting that inner-city parents like these also live in Harlem and Oakland communities, as shown in Jay MacLeod's study, *Ain't No Makin' It*. They are also present in João Costa Vargas's discussion of South Central mothers.[5]

Whatever side they take in the debate, the parents certainly indicate that they strongly believe in the American Dream. Indeed, many of these parents are immigrants, and a few are African American—all have traveled a long, hard road to their seat in this classroom. And in most cases, their kids will represent the first generation in their families to graduate from high school or attend college. They certainly seem determined to have their kids do well. After all, they seem willing to spend four hours (9:00 to 1:00) each Saturday morning listening to lectures like mine and others' on how to change an at-risk kid into an NAI kid who values academic progress and not gang involvement.

Most of these parents seem to be politically attuned to the needs of the community. A number of these parents recognize that their (as they put it) "ghetto" community conditions—trash and other types of garbage—are the fault of the city services and not Danielle, Spencer, or Manuel. Several points should be made here: First, none of the parents use the term *inner city* when referring to their community. It also important to note that while the parents engage in the debate over where to point the blame, throughout the entire time of this study, none of the kids blame their parents or their community. They all place the blame squarely on the shoulders of the city services and lack of protection from the gangs. No one, they say over and over again, cares for them.

Without the support of the NAI staff, the kids lack the kind of cultural capital that the USC students who live near them but not among them tend to possess. Sociologists find that children socialized into the dominant culture have a greater advantage over children not socialized in that culture because schools attempt to reproduce a general set of dominant cultural values and ideas.

Actually, the kids' stories also speak to a set of values and ideas about a culture controlled by gangs. Danielle tells us of the places she avoids: "I avoid streets where there are gangs. Or there are men who stare at me." Spencer agrees: "Yeah. There are places like this everywhere. Like by my school, there are lots of liquor stores and even a few blocks away. It would be okay if they just sold snacks but not liquor stores. Sometimes they drink outside, even if it's illegal to drink in the street." As with most of the kids' comments, I am surprised about Spencer's knowledge of the drinking law. The kids also think, as Spencer's liquor store story indicates, that they are at the mercy of any influence; the kids remember the 50 Cent billboard.

The Painted Doors

When I ask them what things they want to change about their community, they all have similar interests. Danielle wants to change the gang activity around her home, but when she talks with me, mostly she wants to change her landlady's attitude about her family.

> You see these doors on the house? [See Figure 8.9.] I wanted to take a picture of my house—one door is painted white, and our door is painted black. I forgot until I had to turn in my camera. So I took a picture of a house I walked by on the way to school. The lady that owns our house lives next door to us. Her door is painted white,

Figure 8.9

and our door is painted black. We asked her to let us paint our door white, and she said no. She doesn't like us much. We should have a parking space in front of our apartment, but she lets her friends use it, so we have to park way, way, way down the block.

Danielle, a petite, shy twelve-year-old, is so incensed by her landlady's attitude toward her parents that she spends almost half an hour giving us the details of her story. She seems to take the landlady's refusal to let her family paint the door white to mean that her landlady has very little respect for her family—or why would she make a big fuss over painting the door? Perhaps one advantage of being in NAI is that she and the other kids begin to feel that they deserve to be treated better. She wants to change her landlady's personality. "Be better. She's so mean." All of the kids want the people in their community to be more optimistic and "nice." They feel that their neighbors, as Spencer puts it, are "always mad at something or someone." Danielle is another indignant twelve-year-old.

V

Kids' Family Stories

Strain of a Heart

Adults often view middle schoolers as they do younger children, as passive recipients of care, as the focus of adult socialization efforts, and as having little that is constructive to say about family dynamics or social structural factors. However, the views offered by the kids in this study prove otherwise. We hear stories about particular family experiences, and, as in Chapters 4 and 5, the kids recount witnessing events that leave a lasting impression on them. The photos also allow them to talk about how they go about creating or adding to their circle of family care. While they may not tell us all there is to say about these families, the kids do shine a light on larger issues having to do with their need for protection and care. In the telling of these stories, these twelve-to-fifteen-year-olds seem to relish their role as a kind of moral authority figures judging the actions of their families and community.

In describing family life, I recognize that the kids do not and cannot tell the entire story of their lives. For example, we do not learn a great deal about the parents' occupational or educational histories. Nor do we learn much about other family members. But the photos they use seem to trigger a deeply felt need to talk about family experiences.

Annette, Carlos, and Beanna

Twelve-year-old Annette sits with thirteen-year-olds Carlos and Beanna to talk about the photos of their families, and in doing so, they tell stories of parents who, as Annette puts it, "are good people. They are loving and supportive"—although they all admit that their parents work hard and are seldom home before the kids go to bed.

Annette's parents divorced several years ago (she does not remember the exact year), but that does not matter to Annette, since she has a good relationship with both parents. Best of all, Annette has fun when she can "hang out" with her mother at Aunt Mare's house, a few blocks away from her family's apartment. But as with other kid stories (for example, Thomas's bat story in Chapter 7 or Jorge's knife story in Chapter 7), this one evolves into a larger one in which Annette and her family become caught in an incident that clearly affects her. Although Annette cannot establish the time frame—"It may have been last month; I don't remember when"—she recalls an incident that still scares her: "I was at my aunt's house, me and my mother, when out of nowhere, we heard a boom, and then my aunt goes out, and she saw two guys."

CARLOS: Were they throwing things?
BEANNA: Let her tell the story.
ANNETTE: I got scared and heard someone say, "Don't shoot," and then someone said, "Get back into the house," and then my mom called the police. And they were in the house and searching for things, and one of the guys yells, "You only got two minutes before the cops come." They only got seven hundred dollars from my aunt and one hundred dollars from my mom and, like, a dollar from me [*the other kids laugh*], and then they left running, and then the cops came two days after.
CARLOS: Why did they come two days after?
ANNETTE: Because they said that they barely found out, and then we told them that we called them two days ago, and they believed us.

Carlos laughs. He tells the story of his father, who works as a chef, and his mother, who works as a waitress in the same restaurant. Carlos feels like a celebrity: "Mostly every friend my dad has known he works there and knows me and my sisters and we feel kind of special." Perhaps that special feeling has something to do with Carlos's plans for his future: "I just want a job that has to do with business and marketing. I'm not sure what specialty." Carlos, it turns out, is one of the few kids to have a sense of his potential.

Carlos, Beanna, and Annette beam brightly when talking about their parents, reminding me of the smiles I see on the parents' faces when they mention their kids' NAI involvement.

Beanna's father is the only one of the kids' parents to graduate from college, although several parents are enrolled in Santa Monica or Los Angeles City Community College. In this instance, the kids take on the emotional caring for others generally assigned to parents.

I ask, "Carlos, what do you want to say about your family?" Carlos replies:

I don't know how to say it, but some of my family, they envy a lot, so—because we catch them going to a place and doing witchcraft. And I don't know, last time they came to visit us because we haven't seen them in a while, but when I did, I saw my cousin in our bathroom, and they left flowers everywhere. And my cousin put something in my backpack. And my cousin envies a lot. And I got my backpack, and then I found some drugs.

Manuel and three other kids mention their families' belief in witchcraft. "Witchcraft is real for my family," Manuel tells me in another interview. "You guys are not going to believe this, but our family envies us too. They have come from a place where supposedly . . . they do witchcraft. Last time they went to visit us, they placed a cross with needles in our bedrooms. My mom found that someone had done witchcraft on her because she went to someone to read her palm. Yeah. They envy my family." Both Carlos and Manuel think their family members are envious of their success at attending the NAI program. Carlos says it is "because I'm going to go to college, and my cousins can't get into the program," to which Beanna responds, "Don't get me started." Everyone laughs.

Carlos and Manuel may be right. Anthropologist William Madson's study finds that witchcraft plays an important role in Mexican American cultures.[1] The study shows that the practice of witchcraft serves at least four functions for those who hold this belief: (1) it provides a culturally validated explanation for chronic illnesses and death without known causes, (2) it provides an outlet for the release of hatred and resentment, (3) it serves as a means of temporarily reducing anxiety and resentment, and (4) it provides social control of deviance from approved patterns of behavior.

Madson suggests that all of these functions operate as a defense mechanism against pressures from an Anglo society that threatens their sense of cultural cohesiveness. In other words, the use of witchcraft provides these mainly immigrant families with a way to control the world that surrounds them. In Carlos's and Manuel's families, the use of witchcraft permits envious family members to right what they see as the commission of an injustice to their kids. Although none of the Black kids discussed the use of witchcraft in their culture, it is well known that some also practice various forms of witchcraft.

Oscar and Poetia

In a meeting with Willard kids thirteen-year-old Oscar and fourteen-year-old Poetia, we talk about their nine photos of family members. "What did you want to tell me about your family in these photos?" I ask. (See Figure 9.1.) Oscar explains how he helps his mother, who has arthritis, with most of the house cleaning: "I clean her room, the two bathrooms, the living room, the kitchen, the dining room, everything. I get home, like, around 7:00 P.M., and that's when I start to clean and go to sleep, like, around 10:00 P.M. and then I do my homework, like, in the morning. I have no choice [*sighs*]." Poetia's mother, a domestic worker, and her father, a construction worker, are "not home a lot." She points to two photos: one shows her mother posed in front

Figure 9.1

Figure 9.2

of a small stove (see Figure 9.2), and the other shows her father cooking ta-males (see Figure 9.3).

Poetia has also taken a photo of her cousin holding a baby: "My little sis-ter. She's so cute" (see Figure 9.4). In addition, she has taken photos of other cousins and a few distant relations, but there is only one of her father, whom she finds hard to talk to. "My dad has bipolar, so it's like kind of hard to talk to him like you have to know what to say and what not to say because it might trigger something." She goes on to describe a "cool" relationship that "rubs me the wrong way," when her father goes "ballistic" over some minor issue. While this relationship bothers Poetia, she has sympathy for her mother, who likes her job as a seamstress at a local factory, "but sometimes she says her back hurts and that she would like a massage because she has to just sit all day."

Fantasia and Sandee

Two twelve-year-old Latinas, Fantasia and Sandee, are BFFs (kids' lingo for *best friends forever*). They live three blocks from each other; every weekday morning, they walk the five blocks to Forshay Learning Center. But their togetherness story ends since the photos and personal experiences indicate that they live in two different worlds; at least I think so until I learn some time later that both have dropped out of the NAI program at the same time.

Figure 9.3

Figure 9.4

Figure 9.5

Fantasia and Sandee show me their "friendship" photo that a friend took of them (see Figure 9.5). Fantasia informs me that "we actually took many pictures of me." I am not surprised. When I begin the study, I expect that most kids will take photos mostly of themselves and/or friends. After all, why should they care about carrying out my instructions to "take photos to tell me about your life"? It takes a few interviews with the kids before I can come to understand and appreciate their willingness to take this project seriously and how much they have to say about their lives. It turns out that Fantasia and Sandee have only fifteen photos of friends among the fifty photos they took of family and community. In Figure 9.5, dark-haired, tall, and slender Fantasia and blond-streaked, short, and stout Sandee seem glued to each other.

They meet with me one Saturday at 12:30. They arrive ten minutes late and so short of breath that I suspect they ran down the campus lane that leads to the office. They come directly from the Saturday tutorial session for a one-hour interview. Most parents are willing to pick up their kids after the interviews. However, Fantasia's father calls her cell phone just as she sits down for the interview to tell her that she needs to be ready to leave the meeting when he calls again. I ask if I can speak to him, but Fantasia whispers that it is best that she leaves as soon as he calls. It turns out that

Fantasia and Sandee are such great talkers that we cram lots of stories into the twenty-five-minute interview.

I ask Fantasia and Sandee a number of questions about their neighborhoods. Fantasia, speaking first, describes hers as a "lot of cars on the street and lots of people walking around, and some people would say it's dangerous." She sees prostitutes, with "those shorty dresses on, roaming up and down the street and often gangs and some people selling drugs are around there also."

Sandee is one of the few to describe a different kind of neighborhood. "I live near Sixty-Second Street. And she lives on Sixty-Fifth," she says, as if the number reflects the obvious. "Is it better?" I ask. "I don't know. It might be better." Fantasia chimes in as if to support her view of her neighborhood as more dangerous than Sandee's: "My mother has been robbed. Also our house had been robbed seven times, and all our valuables were stolen." Fantasia's mother wants to move to a different city, perhaps to Boston, where their cousins and other relatives live. Her only other family members are in El Salvador or Arizona (she was not sure which). She has never visited them, and they have never visited her. Fantasia says she refuses to leave her neighborhood. She does not want to leave behind her "really really good friends." She takes a breath and says, "Finally, I have friends now." She glances at Sandee.

Sandee's family has lived in their house for twelve years. Her father is trying to earn an associate's degree from Santa Monica Community College, which her eighteen-year-old brother also attends, and plans to transfer into USC and go on to graduate school. And "my mother is going to get her GED and just try to find a job," she says proudly. "She can't find one without a GED."

Fantasia says she does not know "anyone who goes to college." Her mother holds two part-time jobs—one as a flower arranger at a flower shop and the other as a clerk at a real estate office managed by a family friend. "What about your father?" "I don't want to talk about him." We stop for a moment. "Well, let's talk about good stuff. What is your favorite thing to do?" Fantasia pulls at her bright pink sweater that covers a white T-shirt and explains:

> I say school because I can stay at school and not hear my parents fight
> and I can run around with my friends and play. I can let my parents
> fight on their own. Don't want to be there. When I was younger,
> I would stay in my room and listen to loud music and sit in a corner

and rock back and forth like a psycho. I was just crying, but now
I just ignore everything and try to change my life and get on with it.

I ask, "Do you feel safe in this school and feel that people care for you?"
Fantasia says, "I don't know that they care for me. I just don't want to go
home." Sandee touches my hand and says, "I have a confession to make. I
wasn't supposed to come here at all. It wasn't my idea. I don't regret it because there was this teacher." According to the NAI mandate, teachers who
have these students in class and can speak to the kid's potential can recommend them to the NAI director.

Most kids are thrilled to be invited to participate in NAI. It means they
are smart enough to be college bound. But a few, like Fantasia, think that the
recommending teacher does not like her: "Why else would she punish me
by putting me in this program?" In her eyes, the extra time she spends with
NAI tutors, along with time in regular school classes, is a form of punishment.
According to Fantasia, Miss Jackson, the teacher who recommended her, was
"not my favorite, but she told me that I was going to be admitted and had no
choice. She was my history and language teacher. She made us join [*pointing to
Sandee*]. She told us that it was a good opportunity and that we should do it."

Perhaps Fantasia receives so little encouragement from adults in her life
that it makes sense for her to see NAI tutorials as a negative rather than a
positive assessment of their potential. Despite my assurances that teachers
from her school recommend only students who they think will work hard,
Fantasia has her doubts about going to college: "I don't know if I want to go
to college because we [Sandee] have a band, but she [Sandee] wants to go to
college. My dream is to become famous." Fantasia turns down my offer to
have the band play for our research group. "Oh, we suck." The kids' band—
"we call it the Strain of a Heart," Fantasia says—formed only two weeks before our interview. Fantasia and Sandee become engaged in a long discussion
about the possibility of girl rock groups; they mention the Donnas and the
Veronicas, "the biggest girls' groups that are becoming successful." Fantasia
pulls out of the pile on the desk a photo of the posters that cover the walls
of her bedroom (see Figure 9.6). "Guess the name of this group," she says as
she points to the posters of the punk rock group Green Day, which writes
and sings about loneliness, apathy, sex, and drugs. Fantasia wants Strain of a
Heart to be a punk group to follow in the footsteps of Green Day.

A phone call from Fantasia's father interrupts our session. Sandee volunteers to stay for the rest of the interview. After Fantasia leaves, Sandee tells
me that Fantasia has problems with her parents:

Figure 9.6

Fantasia is my friend, but I am worried about her. She tried to commit suicide a couple of months ago. She took some stuff. I don't know what. But her mom found her and took her to the hospital. I think it's her father who doesn't want her to stay in NAI because he thinks she should be home caring for her sisters and not taking time in NAI that's not going to help her.

Fantasia's father is unemployed, and as Sandee puts it, "He gets drunk a lot." In general terms, Fantasia's family situation is not much different from that of other Latinas of her age. Twenty of the fifty-four kids have fathers who are unemployed; the rest have jobs that earn working-class wages.

Latinas: Gender Matters

Fantasia's suicide attempt is not all that surprising to me. A number of studies report on the high suicide rates among Latina kids, including the findings of psychologist Luis Zayas and colleagues, which show that an alarming number of Latina kids contemplate, attempt, or commit suicide. According to this report, in recent years, one of five U.S. Latina kids has attempted suicide, a rate startlingly higher than that of their non-Hispanic peers. Zayas and colleagues go on to report that these suicide rates are higher among Latinas in the United States than in their countries of origin and that the process of American acculturation may be related to higher risk.[2] The researchers suggest that

> traditional gender role socialization, their ethnic identity, and adolescent–parental conflict seem to converge in a suicide attempt. Girls are expected, in traditional Latino cultures, to control their anger and to show their obligation to their families and parents, while struggling with the same developmental issues that other adolescents deal with, such as dating, sexuality, and autonomy and peer-group pressure.[3]

Five NAI Latina middle schoolers report that they know of friends who have made statements about committing suicide. These friends are usually from immigrant families who feel conflicted over their kids' involvement with NAI. Because of the parents' dire economic circumstances, they expect boys to help by earning a living. Latinas are expected to help their mothers tend to the other children or find part-time work after school. Kids like Fantasia often find they are caught in an intense battle with their families over traditional Latino cultural values, unlike American-born girls, who learn a different model about what girls should do, can do, and are permitted to do.[4]

Patricia, a former NAI student and now a USC graduate student, revealed to me that her father could not understand why she needed to attend graduate school: "Wasn't that enough to get a B.A., and now you should get a job?" She explained:

> My father told me it was bad enough I stayed in school and did nothing to help out at home, [but] now I want to waste more time in school. My mother, on the other hand, insisted that I stay in school. She was always telling me, "Don't be like me and get a crummy job because you don't stay in school." The only reason I stayed in school was because my mother made me stay, even though my father was totally against it.

In another study on Latinas and gender issues, Andreana T. Jezzini and her colleagues examine *Marianismo*, which they consider to be frequently underinvestigated in psychological research. *Marianismo* is a Latina gender role phenomenon based on traditional cultural norms and the values of Catholicism. According to Jezzini, this phenomenon, encompassing the concepts of self-sacrifice, passivity, caretaking, duty, honor, sexual morality, and the Latina's role as a mother, is often likened to martyrdom of the Virgin Mary. Additionally, the author's research indicates that there tends to be a high prevalence of depression in Latinas, as well as a high risk of suicide for Latina adolescents.[5]

I find out later that Fantasia does tell a teacher that she is having "wrong thoughts," as Sandee puts it. According to a staff member at her school, the teacher (perhaps in an effort to help Fantasia) alerts a school counselor about Fantasia's situation by sending a fax to the counselor, who leaves the memo on the staff's office desk. Everyone in the office reads the memo, and Fantasia's teacher summons her to the counselor's office. The next week, Fantasia drops out of school, taking Sandee with her.

Antonio and Marcus

EK: Antonio, let's talk about this picture [Figure 9.7].

ANTONIO: Yeah. That's, um, my porch, but we, like, bettered it because when we rented it, it [was] all messed up; there was no roof to cover the beginning because my dog usually sleeps around here, so if it rains, she would get wet, so my parents decide—we decide to fix it up ourselves.

EK: Is this next picture of a bedroom in your house? [See Figure 9.8.]

ANTONIO: Well, yeah, I don't have a dirty house, not that much. I usually do my homework on the couch because that was where I have to sleep because my parents when we moved in, we couldn't have a lot of money so I had to sleep on the couch. But now I sleep on the complete bed and have my own room. And I took this picture of my dogs Princess and Spice lying in my room to show all of my family.

EK (*to the group*): Did you take pictures of your families?

MARCUS: I have two brothers—no, three brothers, with me it's four, and Mom [see Figure 9.9] and Dad [not in the photo]. Dad works for this company about boots. My mom is always at work.

EK: Tell me something about your family.

MARCUS: My sister is annoying. She pulls my hair. My mom is nice, but then she is mean at home. She works as an operator. I don't see her much. She's always running, and then she comes home

Figure 9.7

Figure 9.8

Figure 9.9

late. She works very late, and then when she comes home, I am already asleep. And then I don't really talk to her 'cause she's tired.

EK: How often do you see her?

MARCUS: On Saturdays. Only on Saturdays.

EK: So what else do you want to say about your mom?

MARCUS: Once, my mom worked at a store, and two guys came in. They looked suspicious, so my mom was behind the counter and my grandma was sitting on a chair, and one of these guys came in with a gun. And my mom was nervous and seemed like she was 'bout to faint, and the guy was taller than my grandma. He started to search her, and she doesn't know English that much, so she was like, "No money." When the guy turned to leave, my grandma got a gun that she had a license for, and she was like, "Don't move," and then the guy turned around. She shouted, "I will shoot. I will shoot." And by now the police come. [*Everyone laughs.*]

EK: So, how would you describe a day for you, in your house?

MARCUS: I clean the two bathrooms, the two living rooms, the dining room, everything. My father, sometimes he comes home around eight and makes dinner, and then he has to make calls. I barely see him.

EK (*to Marcus and Antonio*): How would you guys describe your relationship with your dads?

MARCUS: Not good. He has mood swings.

ANTONIO: He needs anger management.

The Skaters, Jeremy and Juan: "Like Family"

Twelve-year-olds Jeremy and Juan live near each other on South Vermont Avenue near USC. Jeremy confesses to liking rock, hip-hop, and funk, and when not doing his homework, he says, "I like skateboarding, and my friends on this street like it too. We go to Arlington Hill because it is a cool place close to my house to go down the hill on our boards."

Jeremy and his family moved into his neighborhood a year ago. The family had to move after a shooting incident near his school that terrified his family. Once they settled into the new neighborhood, Jeremy made some friends, bought a skateboard, and started skating with them. He explains, "I like my new neighborhood better. I can hang out with a lot of my friends. When I lived in my old neighborhood, I would stay in the house and watch a lot of TV, and my mom would always tell me to get up and not be lazy."

I ask Jeremy, "Why did you take this picture of these skateboards?" (see Figure 9.10). He explains:

> They told me to show something that you really like, and I took a picture of all of our boards. And they just look nice. The picture where all our boards are together [I took] because it, like, shows what our boards are like and how they are. All are different because none of us do, like, the same things; we're all sort of different, like family.

Juan's face beams as he describes his photo of his friend (see Figure 9.11): "My friend's name is Jose. See, he, like, be jumping. He's going to jump off the sides, off the sidewalk, and, like, that's where we mostly skate and where we hang out after we stop and we're, like, tired. And that's practically it. It's an element board, and he's, like, an artist." Jeremy says, "Yeah. I like that picture because this is the way I see my friends. We're good friends, and they're never mean to me. Even when I'm mad sometimes, they'll, like, skate with me and talk to me, and I'll calm down."

Juan and Jeremy have few options on where to play games. Both live in small and crowded homes and use skating as a way to socialize ("hang") with

Figure 9.10

Figure 9.11

other kids in the streets in a socially responsible way, according to Jeremy: "My mother said, 'At least you're not in gangs.' I usually keep stuff inside, but on the board, I can let go."

And equally important, although the kids do not make this observation, skateboarding allows them to engage in risk-taking activity. In Juan's photo, Jose is getting ready to skateboard-jump into the street, after which he will jump back onto the sidewalk. These activities carry with them a measure of danger, something that appeals to most adolescents. Both kids speak about skateboarding as having taken on a spiritual quality. Juan, who seems more intense than Jeremy, says that skateboarding "saved my life." Why would twelve-year-old Jeremy say that skateboarding saved his life?

If we are to understand the lives of these kids, his comment is deserving of a sociological analysis. Few sociologists pay attention to the influence that street games and activities—for example, skateboarding—have on the lives of kids, just as years ago, few sociologists understood the spirituality of street basketball or jumping rope to poor Harlem kids. Perhaps skateboarding gives Juan and his friend Jose a way to get free from the overcrowding of a life filled with gangs, violence, and an uncaring school system. I ask Kenny, a USC student and skateboarder, what draws so many kids to the sport. He explains:

> [Adults] don't understand what it's like to be free and unattached from everything. They don't know what it's like to just skate away their problems. You can go wherever you want, and skate pretty much wherever you want. You don't have to listen to what other people say. You are free. Skateboarding is your escape, no matter what your problems are; you just skate and forget even if it is just for the few seconds between the pop of your tail and your wheels returning to the ground.

Kenny describes experiencing that magical moment when all was right with his life. Jeremy and Juan use those moments to develop a strong bond that overcame the loneliness that they felt before they met each other. Perhaps that loneliness comes from seeing their parents mostly on Saturdays or late at night or from living in neighborhoods where the park is considered gang territory. Spencer puts it this way: "Skateboarding makes me feel strong. It saves me from doing bad."

Figure 9.12

The Fake Family Strategy: Juan, Melissa, Jesus, and Cesar

I ask, "What would you like people to know about your pictures?" Juan, pointing to a girl wearing a white shirt who is sitting beside her classmate in a photo, says, "This [girl] with her friend is Amanda. She's my 'play' sister" (see Figure 9.12). "What is a play sister?" I ask. Ten middle schoolers, represented here by Juan, Melissa, Jesus, and Cesar, describe an interesting strategy of creating what they refer to as "fake" or "pretend" families to address needs that echo throughout their stories.

Juan explains, "It's like we all get along so good; they just pretend to be your sister, and, like, you have to get along because you're, like, pretend siblings. And I have a 'pretend' niece, so I had to take pictures of them because they're pretend family." I ask, "How is your pretend niece different from a pretend sister?" Juan responds, "Well, I just have to treat her all nicer because her and I can play-fight and all, but with the younger one, I have to be nice because she's, like, younger than me."

Juan also talks about two friends who are pretending to be brothers. "Like they have names that are so close to each other. They're supposed to be brothers." Marcus used the term "fake parents" to talk about a couple of friends. He refers to one friend as his "fake mommy."

Twenty-five Latinos of the forty-five kids, but none of the Black kids, used the term "fake" or "pretend" family to talk about a peer whom they care for or who cares for them in some way. Twelve-year-old Melissa, who describes her Irish mother and Mexican father as "multiracial," says, "I have a little bit of everyone in me." She talks of having a "fake" mother: "She is my mom but in school." "What does she do as a fake mom?" I ask. Melissa says, "She is always concerned about everybody." According to Melissa, her fake mom, Gelina, who turns fourteen a few days after our interview, makes Melissa behave: "She calms me down. When I get mad, she tells me to stop and be quiet. She helps me with my homework."

Thirteen-year-old Jesus's father works as a janitor for an auto dealership from, as Jesus put it, "7:00 in the morning until, I don't know, but sometimes comes back at 7:00 at night." But he is tired and cranky, he says. Jesus gets lonely sometimes, he admits, because his mother, who babysits her neighbor's four children, is always busy tending to everyone's needs but his. One afternoon, Jesus says:

> See, I live on 103rd Street, and one day, they killed some guy down the street from where I live, and I heard gunshots and some women crying on the street. I called my fake mom because my mom was too busy getting the kids she watches into the bathroom. And I was scared. That was the first phone call to my fake mom. She told me to calm down. The police would come quickly, and everything would go back to normal. The police did come, the women stopped crying, and that was the only bad thing that happened on my street.

Jesus finds out later from Isabel, his fake mom, that the killing is gang related. "I was really glad the community called the police because he had killed a little girl too."

Whenever Jesus feels angry about something, like the time a girl he liked gave him a photo of herself but then took it back and "started backstabbing me a lot," he says, "I called Isabel, and she told me I should have torn up her picture [before I gave it back], and I stopped liking her. That's me hiding behind Isabel" (see Figure 9.13).

In Cesar's case, he says, "my fake dad just came up to me and said, 'I am your father.'" I ask, "What does he do for you as a fake father?" Cesar answers:

> I don't know. Sometimes he comes by me in the schoolyard and asks how I'm doing. But we are really adopted brothers, and I think he's

Figure 9.13

younger than me; he is a month younger than I am. But he is a bit more mature than I am. So, I guess it's okay if he is my fake father.

The kids also expect to become "fake" parents or fake sisters or brothers to other kids as well. Jesus and Melissa are "fake" parents to Elena, who lives next door to Melissa. Melissa and sometimes Jesus help eleven-year-old Elena with her homework and walk with her home from school. Melissa says she helps Elena "sometimes, when I don't have to go to NAI school. I want her to get into NAI, so I help her with everything I can." Cesar is the "pretend" brother to Sara, his thirteen-year-old classmate at Forshay. He explains, "When I see her talking with people I don't like, I walk over and take her by the shoulders to another area."

The fake or pretend family acts much as the extended family reported in Carol Stack's study of the unrelated aunts, uncles, and cousins in Black families.[6] These fictive kin helped each other in time of financial and emotional needs. The fake families created by the kids in this book seem to serve the same purpose, as another arm around their shoulder, so to speak. In Juan's case, he feels the need to be "nicer" to his "pretend" sister than to his own sister because he has the chance to act as the older and wiser brother. Melissa's fake mom is a patient and loving mother who is "concerned" about her, while her "real" mom has to work two jobs to support three children. In Oscar's case, his fake mom makes up for his "real" mom, who is "not home a lot." Poetia's fake mother makes up for Poetia's "cool" relationship with her "real" mom. It is also interesting to note that Jesus's fake mom provides information that keeps him abreast of dangerous incidents in his community—something that all of the kids with fake families seem to relish. And although Wynette did not consider the hooded Black teen who protected her from the other gang members a fake family member, she did feel his arm around her shoulder when he told her to stay put on the bench and warned others to let her get "her learn on" after her teacher made her leave her classroom.

While these fake families may serve the purpose of the extra supportive arm around the kids' shoulders, as Oscar does for his "pretend" sister, it is important to note that in Cesar's case, the father is younger than the son. Therefore, this model of fake or extended family differs from the more age-appropriate model of Black extended family members. Why does the age of these kids' fake family members matter? Perhaps the kids feel that they can trust their peer group, even those who seem to fit the "ghetto thug" image but protected Wynette, because they understand the kids' world. Recall that Jesus learns from his fake mom, Isabel, about the reason for the shooting incident on his street. His real mom would not have access to that gossip line; since Isabel is closer in age to the gang members, it is likely that Jesus believes he can trust that she will have the best information about these kinds of gang-related incidents.

■ ■ ■

Fantasia and Sandee also serve as examples of the power of these peer groups. Sandee tells me that Fantasia confided first in her BFF about her attempted suicide and not in her mother or teacher. Sociologists who study adolescent development find that during adolescence, the peer group plays a larger socialization role than do parents and other adults. That is, during this stage of development, adolescents come to rely on and trust their peers' perceptions of the world. For example, in this community, fourteen-year-old Isabel understands more about gang activity, and Melissa and Cesar believe they know more about school problems than do adults. Yet when Sandee thinks Fantasia needs more help than she can give, she feels she needs to find help for her friend from an adult. But of course, as she may have suspected, the adults botch it up.

Moreover, the kids understand their friends' concerns and the kind of protection they need. The parents may not have a clue. Parents and other adults like Aunt Mare can offer food (limited by the work hours of some parents) and shelter (limited by the small space and number of other family members occupying that space). But the kids need more than supportive parents with limited resources can provide.

In the novel *Lord of the Flies*, author William Golding writes about a group of British schoolboys stuck on a deserted island who try to govern themselves.[7] The story begins just after a plane crash; the boys who have survived the crash find themselves on the island without any adults. Without the usual authority figures to direct them, they must fend for themselves. The novel's disastrous ending demonstrates that kids need some guidance from adults; however, kids still try, as Juan, Jesus, Melissa, Oscar, Cesar, and others do, to govern and protect themselves. When they feel uncared for, isolated, alienated, and rejected, they too take steps to create their own circle of care in order to survive their environment.

10

To Hope for Something

Contextualized Lives

This book is an in-depth study of fifty-four kids' perceptions of inner-city life. These kids see society as failing to grasp the daily challenges they confront or to understand the extent to which they feel shunned, hidden, and forgotten. For Kyle and others, there is an ongoing ambivalence toward the college students' responses to the photograph of the railroad track. This book also addresses the broader implications for social policy.

Three questions come to mind as I think about the kids' stories (the second and third are discussed later in the chapter). First, why would the kids snap photos of the despair and neglect of their community? After all, they are making major changes in their academic achievements. I would have expected a sunnier outlook. Yet another study of children using the camera to capture their lives also had unexpected findings. In the early 1980s, a staff photographer for United Press International (UPI) in Washington, D.C., Jim Hubbard, began documenting the lives of the homeless. He found that when he took pictures of the families, the children often wanted to hold and look through his camera. This innocent curiosity and enthusiasm inspired Hubbard to establish a program that would help homeless children learn photography skills to document their world.[1] Manuel Pastor, who also participated in the program, found that "these kids . . . managed to find the joy and the color in their lives."[2] Whereas one would expect to see photos focusing on the awfulness of homelessness, the kids chose, instead, to see the sunshine in their situations. One of the young homeless participants in the program, when asked why he was photographing his own world, responded, "I'm shooting back."[3] Perhaps the NAI and Willard kids could, in their desire to "shoot back" at their conditions, feel that with their camera work they are also telling us stories about their lives.

As cultural informants, these inner-city kids bring to this study an astute understanding of class and racial inequality. Their photos and interviews constitute a remarkable indictment of mainstream society for its indifference and neglect of the most troubling aspects of inner-city life. The view that "exotic" (Black or Latino) gangs are all that the kids can aspire to was reinforced by the bias I encountered among members of my own academic community. In the view of some, the kids in this study were minimizing their experiences with gangs or lying about their negative feelings about being in gangs, which supports the stereotype that gang affiliation is their most likely outcome.

The interviews show that they want to be seen as responsible kids. Instead, they are greeted with harsh attitudes—labeled as "ghetto thugs" by many adults who, like Bill Cosby, are caught up in a moral outrage over what they see as dysfunctional kids. Never mind that these kids have to live in a hostile inner-city environment not of their making. Never mind the Tennessee Advisory Commission on Intergovernmental Relations report in 2003 stating that in general, students attending school in newer, better facilities score five to seventeen points higher on standardized tests than those attending school in substandard buildings. Or that the quality of the learning environment is known to affect teacher behavior and attitudes about continuing to teach.[4]

The kind of "ghetto thug" labeling that the kids seem intent to disprove creates an image of a stereotypic, homogenous group. But the stereotype's real effect, according to the kids, is to serve as a barrier between inner-city kids and middle-class USC students, between Whites and people of color, and between minority and nonminority kids. In a way this divide acts much like the chain-link fences surrounding the schools and buildings or perhaps like the signs or intersections obscured by bushes that Spencer describes in Chapter 8, "because sometimes you can't even see [what's coming] . . . because . . . the bushes get in the way." The kids are well aware of these barriers but nonetheless challenge them.

Most of the adult authority figures do not seem to care or know how to care for the kids. And the kids? They fear the "ghetto" even more than the

USC students who live on campus. In fact, the survey of six thousand South Los Angeles high school students mentioned in Chapter 5 found that many kids were frightened by violence in school, were deeply dissatisfied with their choices of college preparatory classes, and—perhaps most striking—exhibited symptoms of clinical depression. The survey made the point that South L.A. kids "live in a depressive environment where they feel helpless partly because their choices are so limited." According to the survey's findings, this problem is as much a sociological as a psychological issue.[5] Twelve-year-old Jessica would agree with that analysis: "You see, I stay in my room because I can't go out to play," she says when showing me her photos. The only "haven from a heartless land" is the NAI tutorial program that gives Jessica a sense of order and stability. But everything else in the lives of kids like Jessica reproduces their inequality—for example, Kyle's goal to be a basketball player or machinist despite his math abilities.

Stories of the Scared and Profound

In a few stories, like Fantasia's, there are suicide attempts and, based on J.D.'s demeanor, indicators of depression. Although the kids are working, as one mother put it, "like hell" to achieve an education and change their lives, they still have low self-esteem because they cannot see the benefits of their efforts.

Vincent, a Latino USC undergraduate student, e-mailed me an account of his experiences dealing with the "ghetto thug" label:[6]

During my time at USC I was stopped twice. The first time I was stopped was off of Vermont at the strip mall right across the street from Kap Hall. I was on my way to get lunch and got stopped and asked what I was doing there. The second time was when I was coming back from "The Row" on a Friday night. That time I was asked if I was a student and I responded with "yes." They asked if I had my student ID with me. When they saw that I had it on me and that I had offered to show it to them, they said they didn't need to see it and drove off. It was obvious that it was because of the way that I looked, being that there were a number of students walking around that were not of color.

I personally think that it was a combination of being a minority and the speculation of socioeconomic status. I think that the fact that I was Latino combined with the fact that I didn't look like a "typical" USC student did not help. Both of those times,

I happened to be dressed in loose fitting athletic shorts and a baggy hooded sweatshirt. I was never stopped when I wore the Polo shirt and Jeans, which were usually accompanied by dressy loafers and the USC class ring that I usually wore. If I had to say anything, I would say that it was not just the racial aspect, but that combined with the way I was dressed. In my opinion, dress, like skin color, can send a powerful message. Sometimes I stop and think about the Trayvon Martin case: Would Trayvon, a young African American male, have appeared less threatening to George Zimmerman if he was in a Blazer and Dockers similar to many USC students as opposed to a hoodie?[7]

That label still resonates with this student on an emotional level. Patricia, an NAI graduate and associate researcher on this project, also expresses those feelings, explaining, "I'm still a ghetto thug, even though I'm hoping to go to graduate school for a master's in social work." She goes on to say that she would not have stayed in the program without her mother's insistence:

She wanted a better life for me, not like hers. So, she would scream and yell, "Do you want to be like me?" But I didn't feel I was good enough. Actually, I still don't think I believe I'm in a college program. There is always a reminder, when I go home and see the same problems year after year and when some cop near USC stops me, ask for my driver's license, or ask me where I'm going.

I asked Patricia, "Are you planning to come back to South Central when you graduate from college?" She smiled and said, "Sure, my family is here, my aunts and uncles live here, and my brother, who is now just twelve, is here. Yeah, I want to do something to help my community." It is interesting that Patricia wants to return to South Central to help, despite her degree and her understanding of the area's problems. More often, those who are able to leave these kinds of poor communities generally do.[8]

• • •

Throughout this book, the kids, acting as informants, use their photos to show us how they see their lives and to contest the adult authority that attempts to restrict and restrain them. They credit only a few with caring for them. The rest do not seem to care or to know how to care for these kids. The kids have shown us through photos and in their interviews the connection between institutional oppression and relational support. They develop intense relationships with the after-school programs they attend and create "fake" family relationships with peers. They develop their strategies as a way to make up for the poverty of their relationships with those who have turned their backs on these inner-city kids. As one observer put it, "These same children of South Central Los Angeles are likely to have cold lives. A ceiling is placed on their dreams by an environment that taught individuals to expect little and to hope for nothing."[9]

You can see the "hope for nothing" in the photos depicting the sadness of the community: the wrecked cars parked in driveways, the chain-link fences surrounding schools, the piles of trash on the street, the dirty school toilets, and the teachers who stand against blackboards while security guards isolate them from their students.

"Hey, I want to do something with my life," twelve-year-old Cesar tells me. Never mind those gloomy photos; when you look closely, you also see hope in the photos taken of family, friends, teachers, classmates, and neighborhoods. Perhaps the hope for "something" comes from the care and support of the NAI program and from the kids' success in the program. In an earlier chapter, Abby is certainly excited about being in the program. What she sees is the safety net provided by the program. Other kids say that without the resources of the NAI program, they are not hopeful about the possibility of attending college. I can see the smiles on Kyle's and Cesar's faces when they walk onto campus or when they are being tutored by some students in my classes. These volunteer students have reported how much they and the kids enjoy the tutoring sessions. These kids do not back away or drop out. Rather, they use their critical skills and their five-dollar disposable camera to make statements about institutional care. Wynette, DeWayne, and Nace offer critiques of institutional care, while Cesar uses his photos to talk about his teacher's burrito and adult irresponsibility. All of them mention their need to trust adults and to feel trusted by adults whom they hold responsible for their community's social problems.

You can also see their hope for something in the numerous photographs they take of family, friends, classmates, and neighborhood games. You can also see the hope for something in the many photos they take of various places on the USC campus. Each NAI kid has taken at least five photos of something related to USC: a kid standing in front of a campus building (Figure 10.1); a jacket with USC's logo covering a chair next to Nordeen, a former NAI volunteer and USC graduate, who is doing classwork in a campus classroom (Figure 10.2); a USC parade (Figure 10.3; the photo is blurry,

Figure 10.1

Figure 10.2

Figure 10.3

but Spencer is excited about capturing the parade for this project); and thirteen-year-old Kaylee with a pom-pom on her head (Figure 10.4). Some have suggested that Kaylee's pom-pom photo best represents the NAI kids' emotional attachment to NAI and USC.

I consider more than simply the kids' responses to racism and inequality. The second question that comes to mind as I think about the kids' stories has to do with how to determine how institutions and adults involved in kids' lives perpetuate their feelings of worthlessness. Michael Schwalbe argues succinctly that those who write the rules have the economic and political power to subjugate the vulnerable, even if they do not have the explicit intent of being prejudiced or discriminating against others.[10] But Schwalbe does not go far enough. This study suggests that often those adults with limited power—in this case, teachers, school administrators, counselors, and security guards, to mention only a few, and often people of color—capitulate to the rules, norms, and values that produce their moral outrage about these kids and, by doing so, reinforce institutional inequality as so clearly pointed out by Kyle, Cesar, DeWayne, and others.

The kids' photographs, along with their stories, give us a keen sense of how inequality is produced—by grouping people by race and class into a segregated and deprived community with a weak infrastructure. Inequality

Figure 10.4

is therefore reproduced when the kids are bound together under the label "ghetto thug," although these kids are working, as noted previously by one mother, "like hell" to achieve an education. That label still resonates with them on an emotional level—which is why they turned their lenses on their community, school, and family experiences.

Based on the interviews and photos, the kids in this study are gaining more than an academic education; they are also learning a thing or two about their worthiness. From their point of view, caring for the environment of inner-city kids is not high on the school's or anyone's agenda. If we expect these kids to become competent members of society—and here I mean not just by improving their math and English skills—we must demonstrate competence in helping them develop what Katherine Call refers to as the "possible selves."[11] In other words, these kids, who have an opportunity to attend college if they continue with their academic pursuits, are also asking to become emotionally competent—to care and to be cared for by the very adults who require so much of them: behaving well, completing homework, passing exams, respecting the school staff, and keeping the bathrooms clean. Photos taken by Abby, J.D., Jessica, and other kids say that emotional caring should be the basis for adolescence to develop competency in life. The many photos of kids in white T-shirts and displaying gang signs show us that the signs of another culture await them if their school does not recognize their needs.

Interestingly, Elise Boulding's study can serve as a warning. Boulding's findings show that the age of children may influence their degree and variety of empathy and nurturing. If anything, a wider and more imaginative range of caring acts is reported from kids ages five and younger than from older kids. Here Boulding refers to the tendency of the young to act in caring ways; however, as children age, they appear to lose the ability to feel empathy toward others.[12] Studies on gang violence and peer group influence show that middle and high school kids can be cruel and commit harmful acts.[13] Boulding's research shows that middle schoolers who feel that the only environment they know does not care for them, as do these inner-city kids, are likely to carry those feelings with them into adulthood, perhaps becoming the angry employee or employer or the absentee or abusive parent.[14]

Hillary Rodham Clinton opens her book *It Takes a Village: And Other Lessons Children Teach Us* with a comment that applies to these kids:

> Children are not rugged individualists. They depend on the adults they know and on thousands more who make decisions every day that affects their well-being. All of us, whether we acknowledge it or not, are responsible for deciding whether or not our children are raised in a nation that doesn't just respond to family values, but values families and children.[15]

We assume that Clinton is referring to children younger than middle schoolers. DeWayne may be older and taller and talk about loftier matters than young children, but he also wants adults to take responsibility for loving and caring for him. It does takes a village but only if that village can improve the school system, decrease the isolation of the kids from the larger city of Los Angeles, and create more centers where kids can go to "get their learn on." Perhaps Robert Sampson's suggestion that it may take more than a village to raise kids—in this case, middle schoolers, a group that is largely ignored in studies that focus mainly on the care of young children—is accurate. Kids also need an intensive, emotional bond that allows adults to be held responsible for the well-being of children at all levels.[16] This research shows that kids who feel that the only environment they know does not care for them, as these inner-city kids do, may choose the gang.[17] Recall the photo of the finger pose of the NAI group in Chapter 5 (Figure 5.3).

The third question—and what I consider to be the most important sociological one—has to do with how we can change the general perceptions and lives of inner-city kids so that they can be seen as full human beings and not as hooded animals straight out of the 'hood. We need to understand the process by which social change takes place. We can begin with learning to see their lives from their perspective. We can also create a safe afterschool program based on the NAI model for all inner-city children in need. According to both NAI and Willard kids, it does take a village to create a supportive environment that they can use as a safe haven from the gangs, drugs, and violence they see on a daily basis.

NAI kids may have found their safe haven. When I talked to Joanne Gray and others about the NAI program, they all say they know kids that could benefit from the program. They also asked if I could help them place kids they know into the program, believing that I had more clout than I did. The NAI program is open only to kids who attend five local schools surrounding the USC area. Perhaps a new way to see these kids would allow us to give new meaning to their lives, and that sentiment would give us a charge to give them more care and more love. We can use the model of NAI as a start. The program is based on the notion that inner-city students can achieve if given the chance—and not only the best and brightest but those who are at risk for dropping out of the educational system, as were Fantasia and Sandee.

The NAI program requires parents' attendance at parent meetings and parenting classes. The students are required to create a pool of friends from the NAI group, and as Kyle said, the program has a positive impact on behavior. The USC campus feels safe, and Cesar sums up what other NAI kids say about the USC students who volunteer for NAI: "They are really great with us. I want to go to USC." Love and care and the possibility that they too will succeed gives the kids a way to expect more because they see more coming their way. However, Wynette's school stories warn us that despite the possibility of a way out, there are still those who want to keep the kids locked into their current conditions by stamping them with the "ghetto thug" image.

We need to understand the process by which social change takes place, and the kids in this study tell us a great deal about this process. It takes, if DeWayne has his way, a place to do homework, meet others, watch television, and eat pizza. But he wants more. He wants his mother to spend time with him.

. . .

In my previous study of NAI kids, I quote Erik Erikson's interest in the psychological stages of children's development; this is also an issue relevant to this study. Erikson emphasizes a psychosocial stage in which a sense of trust and security has to be established between the child and adult. Trust and security are defined as a "feeling of physical comfort and a minimal amount of fear and apprehension about the future." Children who are able to feel trust and security in their surroundings will expect the world to be a "good and pleasant place to live."[18] I suggest that kids who do not have a good and pleasant place to live will develop behavior or attitude problems in school (as well as in other areas) and find it difficult to change them.[19]

It is important, therefore, to emphasize in this study how the kids grapple with their emotional feelings about their status in this society so that they learn how to develop their own strategies to compensate for their lack of a safe haven in the larger social world. Kids become involved in gangs and teenage girls have babies as ways to make up for the social support missing in their lives. These kids, in both the NAI and Willard programs, use the photos to teach us how to see the world. What is unusual and surprising is their ability to see the structural factors in ways that say they feel uncared for. They do not blame their parents. Instead, they understand and take aim at rats in the lunchroom, garbage piles, and badly painted house doors, all social problems that most adults would not expect kids of this age to be aware of or to care about. Their level of awareness is the most interesting finding; second is their strong desire to see these problems in almost adult terms. For example, twelve-year-old middle schooler Jessica was extremely offended about her school's dirty bathrooms, and fourteen-year-old J.D. was concerned about uncaring teachers.

In this book, I have let the kids show us how they see their lives. But this book is not just about how they see their lives; it raises questions about how we see kids who want the same as everyone else—a safe place to live, one in which they can feel protected from being exposed to all kinds of violence that may, in the long run, engulf them because they feel left out of mainstream life.

The kids' photos and interviews indicate that they are grappling with these issues. During one interview with Carlos and Kyle, I point to a photo of a chain-link fence that, although I have seen at least twenty-five photos of these fences, I assume Carlos has taken simply as a lark (see Figure 10.5).

EK: Why did you take this picture of a chain-link fence in front of garbage cans?

Figure 10.5

CARLOS: I don't know. Maybe because my friends are always joking about there is so much fences in my block, we kinda feel we live our lives behind them.

KYLE: You could look at it from two sides. If you're on one side of the fence, you could say you're on the outside looking in, as if you're not part of their world. You look at it from the other, you can say you're trapped on the inside in your own home.

My main focus was on kids' perceptions of the impact of context/environment on their own lives and by extension how the psychosocial contexts—family, school, work, and neighborhood—affect kids' cognition, health, decision making, and self-esteem. The research findings provide a study of Los Angeles inner-city adolescents that deepens and enriches current theory by making explicit the complexities surrounding the lives of inner-city minority kids. Director Tim Burton's poem in his book of poetry, *The Melancholy Death of Oyster Boy and Other Stories*, comes to mind as I hear Carlos's and Kyle's comments that they are not part of the world—a sentiment expressed by all of the kids.

And Robot boy grew up to be a young man,
though he was often mistaken for a garbage can.[20]

These kids are asking for more than to succeed academically. In their view, it is not enough to gain an education, learn a trade, and make a decent wage. It is equally important, they seem to say, that kids learn caring skills and that they learn them from caring adults so they grow up in a society that cares for them and in which they learn to care for others. And where else will they learn those skills but from those who serve as authority figures in their lives?

I argue that kids like those in this study are largely ignored in favor of the more exotic gang culture stereotypically associated with South Central L.A. The proliferation of studies on inner-city kids involved in gang violence, on drugs, or in prison further exacerbates institutional bias against aspiring kids with goals not associated with gang membership or whose affiliations are few or nonexistent. In addition, ignoring and/or dismissing kids like those in this study while focusing on gang culture reinforces the perception that no other population exists. These kids are generally ignored not only in the research on inner-city kids but also by many federally and privately funded programs that focus on gangs, students with special needs, or those considered to be exceptional students.

These inner-city kids have suffered from a great deal of neglect resulting from both a lack of institutional support and insufficient care by adults in authority. The kids use their photographs and interviews to speak of that neglect and to refute the dysfunctional image of "ghetto thug" by revealing a tremendous number of social and structural inequalities previously over-looked in other literature on inner-city kids.

Kids growing up in high-poverty neighborhoods, with extreme racial and economic segregation and inadequate public services—police, schools, sanitation, grocery stores—are at risk for negative outcomes, including poor physical and mental health, cognitive delays, risky sexual behavior, and delinquency. The negative consequences for these kids' lives—and for so-ciety—are severe; they are more likely than those who grow up in other com-munities to drop out of high school, become involved in gangs, and become teen parents, and they are less likely to be employed as adults.[21]

There has also been comparatively little research on the ways that the neighborhoods where children live affect their transitions to adulthood or on the characteristics other than poverty that may influence their develop-ment. Even fewer programs or policies have tried to address the community mechanisms that may be causing such bad outcomes. Rather, most research and policy attention concentrates on the individual child, the child's family, and school settings, touching on many points along the path to adulthood beginning with pregnancy planning and continuing through pre- and post-natal care, early childhood development, schooling, and the myriad challenges confronting adolescents as they transition into adulthood. As a result, policies aimed at helping disadvantaged children and youth tend to focus on individual families and children and on school-based reforms.

. . .

These kids and their photos tell a larger story about the ghetto and those who live there, often in shame. This story is about the parents, some of whom hardly speak English but are ready to take some kind of action to get the school bathrooms fixed or the garbage picked up, if only they can get the time away from working two jobs or long hours or save up enough money to buy a car to get around. This story is also about adults who have taken on the individualist ideology and believe that kids could do better in school, if only they would take off their hoods and get back to school. This story is about adults who took a hard look at the kids' situation and understood that these kids, who benefit from programs like NAI and Willard, have a chance to achieve their dream—"to do something," as Cesar declares. We all know the stories of those kids who do not have that chance.[22]

By moving beyond the stories about the culture of poverty and stereotypes about "ghetto thugs" or inner-city problem kids, I show how a group of twelve-to-fifteen-year-old kids have been able to use photos to have their say about the structural forces and relational impoverishment in their immediate surroundings. As mentioned previously, Pierre Bourdieu's theory of achievement raises significant questions for this research: Can an inner-city child aspire to achieve and transcend the limitations of his or her objective probabilities? Kyle, Wynette, and the other kids are certainly trying to do so. As I said in other work, social reproduction theory assumes that those in power will reproduce the system that gave them power. This theory can be applied to this community of inner-city kids inversely: those not in power will reproduce a powerless society. Social reproduction theory also argues that schools are not institutions of equal opportunity but mechanisms for perpetuating social inequality.

But this study reveals that the kids perceived themselves as gaining social and cultural capital resources as a result of their participation in the after-school programs. The kids' discussion of these programs indicate that the kids' staff and parent relationships are built around the idea of care as the key component that facilitates the process of the kids' developing, acquiring, and ultimately activating the social and cultural capital resources they need to connect their experiences as inner-city kids with their photos.

The stories the kids tell us through photographs and in-depth interviews present an alternative perspective of their world. Some stories and photos have a tremendous emotional impact on the teller—for example, Wynette's stories about the teacher who refused to let her stay in the classroom when she was scared and the gangster who gave her permission to sit on the school bench. Some (such as Cesar's burrito story) are funny in catching the absurdity of the person or event. Others (such as the stories about fake families) are love stories about parents and friends.

In this book, Kyle, J.D., and others have their chance to respond to the stereotypes and to raise questions about what it means to live in South Central through stories and photos that voice the shame and hurt the kids feel about some condition, problem, or authority figure. In some cases, the kids speak to one aspect of life in South Central, while the photos speak to another aspect. When these stories and photos are woven together—for example, the photos of wrecked cars in need of repair and the insufferable bathroom conditions, all clearly signs of poverty—we see the physical reality of inner-city life and the structural forces at play. The physical reality in those photos serves as a backdrop for the personal dramas told in stories of gangs, gunshots, and carjackings. Taken together, the photos and what this group of kids have tried to tell us in their stories have provided what they see as the reality of life for inner-city kids living in South Central Los Angeles. This story is not only about inner-city kids. It is also about how we as a society, with our misguided perceptions, withhold care from a vulnerable population.

Appendix A

Participants by Race/Ethnicity, Gender, and Age

Race/Ethnicity	Girls	Boys	Age 12	Age 13	Age 14	Age 15	Totals
Neighborhood Academic Initiative students							
Latino	13	20	12	14	6	4	33
Black	2	4	2	2	1	1	6
Willard After-School Program students							
Black	7	8	—	3	2	10	15

Appendix B

University of Southern California Neighborhood Academic Initiative Program Graduate Survey, 1997–2011

	1997	%	1998	%	1999	%
Total graduates	**46**		**55**		**39**	
USC	22	47.8	25	45.5	16	41.0
Other private 4-year college	0	0	2	3.6	5	12.8
UC system	2	4.3	3	5.5	3	7.7
Cal State system	2	4.3	5	9.1	5	12.8
Other state systems	1	2.2	0	0	2	5.1
Total enrollment of 4-year colleges	**27**	**58.7**	**35**	**63.6**	**31**	**79.5**
Community college (transfer to USC as sophomores)*	15	32.6	14	25.5	7	17.9
Vocational college	0	0	3	5.5	0	0
Total enrollment of postsecondary education	**42**	**91.3**	**52**	**94.5**	**38**	**97.4**
Unknown/working/military	4	8.7	3	5.5	2	5.1

	2005	%	2006	%	2007	%
Total graduates	**42**		**42**		**36**	
USC	12	28.6	7	16.7	10	27.8
Other private 4-year college	6	14.3	6	14.3	4	11.1
UC system	8	19.0	13	31.0	16	44.4
Cal State system	6	14.3	11	26.2	5	13.9
Other state systems	0	0	1	2.4	0	0
Total enrollment of 4-year colleges	**32**	**76.2**	**37**	**88.0**	**35**	**97.2**
Community college (transfer to USC as sophomores)*	10	23.8	4	9.5	1	2.8
Vocational college	0	0	0	0	0	0
Total enrollment of postsecondary education	**42**	**100**	**42**	**100**	**36**	**100**
Unknown/working/military	0	0	0	0	0	0

* As part of the USC Scholarship, students who are not admitted as freshmen to USC but graduate in good standing and go on to complete a course of study at a selected two-year college are eligible to transfer in to the university as sophomores. These students are then eligible to receive five semesters of the NAI scholarship to complete their undergraduate degree.

2000	%	2001	%	2002	%	2003	%	2004	%
45		46		32		32		33	
8	17.8	11	23.9	4	12.5	15	46.9	12	36.4
10	22.2	9	19.6	8	25.0	3	9.4	3	9.1
10	22.2	9	19.6	5	15.6	8	25.0	8	24.2
11	24.4	10	21.7	5	15.6	4	12.5	7	21.2
2	4.4	0	0	0	0	2	6.2	0	0
41	91.1	39	84.8	22	68.8	32	100	30	90.9
2	4.4	4	8.7	8	25	0	0	3	9.1
0	0	0	0	1	3.1	0	0	0	0
43	95.6	43	93.5	31	96.9	32	100	33	100
2	4.4	2	4.3	1	3.1	0	0	0	0

2008	%	2009	%	2010	%	2011	%	Total, 1997–2011	Total %, 1997–2011
41		44		56		46		635	
20	48.8	15	34.1	27	48.2	12	26.1	216	34
3	7.3	3	6.8	0	0	7	15.2	63	10
3	7.3	13	29.5	9	16.1	11	23.9	121	19
9	22.0	7	15.9	6	10.7	6	13.0	99	16
0	0	0	0	0	0	0	0	8	1
36	87.8	38	86.4	42	75.0	36	78.3	513	82
5	12.2	6	13.6	13	23.2	10	21.7	102	16
0	0	0	0	1	1.8	0	0	5	<1
41	100	44	100	56	100	46	100	621	98
0	0	0	0	0	0	0	0	14	2

Appendix C

Assignments and Questionnaire

PHOTO ASSIGNMENTS:

Shoot pictures of your neighborhood, favorite places, least favorite places, home, friends, schools, and homework assignments you like and do not like.

SOME SUGGESTIONS:

Take pictures of anything you want to show me about your experiences.

You do not have to take pictures of anything that looks dangerous.

You can change your mind about taking pictures.

You can change your mind about pictures you take but no longer want to show them.

You can throw the camera away if you want, or if you lose it, you will be given another one if you want it.

Do not take pictures of anyone you know who may be a gang member.

INTERVIEW QUESTIONS:

What is it you want to say about your life based on these pictures?

What pictures do you like best? Least?

What about the stuff you took but didn't like? Do you want to talk about that stuff?

Notes

CHAPTER 1

1. For a map of and general statistics on South Central Los Angeles, see http://projects.latimes.com/mapping-la/neighborhoods/neighborhood/historic-south-central.

2. I refer to the photographs as "pictures" in discussions with the kids.

3. See Appendix A for a table of the teen participants by race/ethnicity, gender, and age.

4. "Historic South-Central," *Los Angeles Times*, 2012, available at http://projects.latimes.com/mapping-la/neighborhoods/neighborhood/historic-south-central/#population.

5. See NAI's web page at http://communities.usc.edu/education/nai.html.

6. Elaine Bell Kaplan, "'It's Going Good': Inner-City Black and Latino Adolescents' Perceptions about Achieving an Education," *Urban Education* 34, no. 2 (1999): 181–213. In this article, a pseudonym was used in place of NAI's name.

7. Shoshana Polansky, "Routes to Inner-City College Preparatory Success: University of Southern California Neighborhood Academic Initiative," unpublished honors thesis, University of Southern California, 2012.

8. Quoted in Polansky, "Routes to Inner-City College Preparatory Success," 2.

9. See Appendix B for the NAI Graduate Survey.

10. Deborah Meier, "A Talk to Teachers," *Dissent* (Winter 1994): 80–87.

11. John U. Ogbu, *Black American Students in an Affluent Suburb: A Study of Academic Disengagement* (Mahwah, NJ: Lawrence Erlbaum, 2003).

12. Ibid. Also see, for example, Allen Scott and E. Richard Brown, *South-Central Los Angeles: Anatomy of an Urban Crisis* (Berkeley: University of California Press, 1983); Miles Corwin, *And Still We Rise: The Trials and Triumphs of Twelve Gifted Inner-City Students* (New York: HarperPerennial, 1997); and João H. Costa Vargas, *Catching*

Hell in the City of Angels: Life and Meanings of Blackness in South Central Los Angeles (Minneapolis: University of Minnesota Press, 2006).

13. For research data on drive-bys, see Violence Policy Center, "Drive-by America," July 2007, available at http://www.vpc.org/studies/driveby.pdf.

14. Pit bulls are popular among many South Central residents because they are often used for dogfighting, which can be profitable for their owners. See Eileen Fleming, "Animal Control Officers Must Deal with Pit Bulls, the Hype," *Lodi News-Sentinel*, June 25, 1987, available at http://news.google.com/newspapers?id=DbEzAAAAIBAJ&sjid=jDIHAAAAIBAJ&pg=6837,7380973&dq=why+do+people+buy+pitbulls&hl=en.

15. See, for example, Terry Williams and William Kornblum, *Growing Up Poor* (Lexington, MA: Lexington Books, 1985); Elijah Anderson, *Streetwise* (Chicago: University of Chicago Press, 1999); and Jay MacLeod, *Ain't No Makin' It: Aspirations and Attainment in a Low-Income Neighborhood* (Boulder, CO: Westview Press, 2008). For studies on the Los Angeles inner-city community, see, for example, Scott and Brown, *South-Central Los Angeles*; Corwin, *And Still We Rise*; and Vargas, *Catching Hell*.

16. MacLeod, *Ain't No Makin' It*, 2.

17. Mitchell Duneier, *Sidewalk* (New York: Farrar, Straus and Giroux, 1999), 12.

18. Ibid.

19. Mitchell Landsberg, "Some California Dropouts Finish High School but Don't Succeed Beyond, Study Finds," *Los Angeles Times*, September 12, 2008, 25.

20. Drug kingpin Frank Lucas smuggled heroin into Harlem during the 1970s by buying drugs from Vietnamese drug lords and hiding the stash inside the coffins of American soldiers returning from Vietnam. His rise to drug lord is depicted in the movie *American Gangster*.

21. See David Hajdu, *Lush Life: A Biography of Billy Strayhorn* (New York: Farrar, Straus and Giroux, 1996).

22. Jill Leovy, "Community Struggles in Anonymity," *Los Angeles Times*, July 7, 2008, available at http://articles.latimes.com/2008/jul/07/local/me-nameless7.

23. Rosemary V. Barnett and Sally Moore, "Helping Teens Answer the Question 'Who Am I?': Moral Development in Adolescents," February 2009, available at http://edis.ifas.ufl.edu/fy964.

24. Norman K. Denzin, *On Understanding Emotion* (Piscataway, NJ: Transaction, 2007).

CHAPTER 2

1. Jay MacLeod, *Ain't No Makin' It: Aspirations and Attainment in a Low-Income Neighborhood*, 3rd ed. (Norwood, MA: Westwood Press, 2009), 8.

2. *Born into Brothels: Calcutta's Red Light Kids*, directed by Zana Briski and Ross Kaufman (2004).

3. Caroline Wang and Mary Ann Burris, "Photovoice: Concept, Methodology, and Use for Participatory Needs Assessment," *Health Education and Behavior* 24, no. 3 (1997): 369–387.

4. Nina Wallerstein and Edward Bernstein, "Empowerment Education: Freire's Ideas Adapted to Health Education," *Health Education and Behavior* 15, no. 4 (1988): 379–394.

5. See "Photovoice," available at http://people.umass.edu/afeldman/Photovoice .htm (accessed June 13, 2011).

6. "Vision and Mission," *PhotoVoice*, 2012, available at http://www.photovoice.org/ about/info/vision-and-mission.

7. Wallerstein and Bernstein, "Empowerment Education."

8. I also created an undergraduate course, Visual Sociology of the Urban Area and Its Residents, based on this methodology.

9. Wang and Burris, "Photovoice."

10. Clifford Geertz, *The Interpretation of Culture* (New York: Basic Books, 1973). Also see Safe Kids Worldwide, "Photovoice: Children's Perspectives on Road Traffic Safety in Ten Countries," October 2, 2012, available at http://www.walk21.com/ papers/45%29%20PHOTOVOICE%20PRESENTATION%20-%20Walk21.pdf.

11. Christine Cordone, personal communication with author, 2009–2012.

12. Quoted in Richard Bolduc, "Art Therapy Helps Children Express Their Emotions," *Family Anatomy*, January 28, 2009, available at http://www.familyanatomy .com/2009/01/28/art-therapy-helps-children-express-their-emotions/. Also see Michael Day and Al Hurwitz, *Children and Their Art: Art Education for Elementary and Middle Schools* (Boston: Wadsworth, 2011)

13. See Appendix C for the questionnaire.

14. C. Wright Mills, *The Sociological Imagination* (New York: Oxford University Press, 1956).

15. W. I. Thomas, *The Child in America: Behavior Problems and Programs* (New York: Knopf, 1928), 571–572.

CHAPTER 3

1. See JGONOT, "Sprawl L.A.: The Impact of Sprawl in Los Angeles—Part 1," *ArchLand*, July 19, 2011, available at http://archlandblog.com/?p=322.

2. See Marla Cone, "A Toxic Tour: Neighborhoods Struggle with Health Threats from Traffic Pollution," *Environmental Health News*, October 7, 2011, available at http://www.environmentalhealthnews.org/ehs/news/2011/1008a-toxic-tour-of-la.

3. See Carolyn Kellogg, "'La-La Land,' Now the Dictionary Definition of Los Angeles," *Los Angeles Times*, March 25, 2011, available at http://latimesblogs.latimes .com/jacketcopy/2011/03/la-la-land-now-the-dictionary-definition-of-los-angeles.html; "Los Angeles," *Wikipedia*, n.d., available at http://en.wikipedia.org/wiki/Los_Angeles (accessed January 22, 2013); "The Entertainment Capital of the World," *Wikipedia*, n.d., available at http://en.wikipedia.org/wiki/The_Entertainment_Capital_of_the_World (accessed January 22, 2013); and "Olympic History," *WorldAtlas*, n.d., available at http://www.worldatlas.com/aatlas/infopage/olympic.htm (accessed January 22, 2013).

4. Michael Matsunaga, "Concentrated Poverty Neighborhoods in Los Angeles," 2010 available at http://www.lachamber.com/clientuploads/LUCH_committee/ 052610_ConcentratedPoverty.pdf.

5. Ibid., 1.

6. Ibid.

7. Allen Scott and E. Richard Brown, *South-Central Los Angeles: Anatomy of an Urban Crisis* (Berkeley: University of California Press, 1983).

8. "Park History," *Exposition Park*, 2007, available at http://www.expositionpark .org/park-history.

9. See "Manual Arts High School Alumni," available at http://manualartshigh school.org/ (accessed August 1, 2011).

10. João H. Costa Vargas, *Catching Hell in the City of Angels: Life and Meanings of Blackness in South Central Los Angeles* (Minneapolis: University of Minnesota Press, 2006).

11. Scott and Brown, *South-Central Los Angeles*.

12. Ibid., 23. In 1945, a Black family by the name of Shelley purchased a house in St. Louis, Missouri. At the time of purchase, they were unaware that a restrictive covenant had been in place on the property since 1911. The restrictive covenant barred "people of the Negro or Mongolian Race" from owning the property. Neighbors sued to restrain the Shelleys from taking possession of the property they had purchased. The Supreme Court of Missouri held that the covenant was enforceable against the purchasers because the covenant was a purely private agreement between the original parties thereto, which ran with the land and was enforceable against subsequent owners. Ibid.

13. "South Los Angeles," *Wikipedia*, n.d., available at http://en.wikipedia.org/ wiki/South_Los_Angeles (accessed January 29, 2013); "Spook Hunters," *Wikipedia*, n.d., available at http://en.wikipedia.org/wiki/Spook_Hunters (accessed January 29, 2013).

14. "South Los Angeles."

15. "Gangs," Los Angeles Police Department, n.d., available at http://www.lapdon line.org/get_informed/content_basic_view/1396 (accessed January 29, 2013).

16. "Gang," *Wikipedia*, n.d., available at http://en.wikipedia.org/wiki/Gang (accessed January 29, 2013).

17. Tom Hayden, *Street Wars: Gangs and the Future of Violence* (New York: New Press, 2006).

18. Judith Greene and Kevin Pranis, "Gangs in Los Angeles," in *Gang Wars: The Failure of Enforcement Tactics and the Need for Effective Public Safety Strategies*, 25–30 (Washington, DC: Justice Policy Institute), available at http://www.justicepolicy.org/ images/upload/07–07_REP_GangWars_GC-PS-AC-JJ.pdf.

19. Scott Gold, "Hoping Peace Moves In," *Los Angeles Times*, July 14, 2009, 5.

20. Mandalit del Barco, "Los Angeles Cracks Down on Gangs," *NPR*, January 19, 2007, available at http://www.npr.org/templates/story/story.php?storyId=6920872.

21. Scott and Brown, *South-Central Los Angeles*.

2. See Josh Kun, "The Kids Are New, but the Block Isn't," *Los Angeles Times*, 11, 2006, available at http://articles.latimes.com/2006/jun/11/entertainment/ca- p11. The title of this chapter is the title of a 1996 Wayans brothers film parodying *n the Hood* and similar films.

3. Joel Rubin, "L.A. Crime Tally Falls at a Slower Rate," *Los Angeles Times*, nber 28, 2012, 1.

4. Loic J. D. Wacquant and William Julius Wilson, "The Cost of Racial and Class sion in the Inner City," *Annals of the American Academy of Political and Social e* 501, no. 1 (1989): 8–25.

5. Elijah Anderson, *Codes of the Street: Decency, Violence, and the Moral Life of the City* (New York: Norton, 1999), 185.

26. Ibid., 4.

27. Ibid., 185.

28. Valerie Hansen, "American Children Eating Fast Food Leads to Health Problems," *Yahoo! Voices*, November 10, 2005, available at http://www.associatedcontent.com/article/13227/american_children_eating_fast_food_pg2.html?cat=5.

29. "Film Studio Removes Controversial 50 Cent Billboard," StarPulse.com, October 28, 2005, available at http://www.starpulse.com/news/index.php/2005/10/28/film_studio_removes_controversial_50_cen.

30. "'Killer King' L.A. Hospital in Peril," CBS News, February 11, 2009, available at http://www.cbsnews.com/2100-201_162-2965723.html.

31. Tracy Weber, Charles Ornstein, and Mitchell Landsberg, "Deadly Errors and Politics Betray a Hospital's Promise," *Los Angeles Times*, December 5, 2004, available at http://articles.latimes.com/2004/dec/05/local/la-me-kdday1dec05.

32. "'Killer King' L.A. Hospital in Peril."

33. "Woman Dies in ER after 911 Dispatchers Refuse to Help Caller," KSDK.com, June 15, 2007, available at http://www.ksdk.com/news/story.aspx?storyid=121954.

34. Weber, Ornstein, and Landsberg, "Deadly Errors."

35. Jack Leonard, "King-Harbor Inspection Report Released," *Los Angeles Times*, August 14, 2007, available at http://www.latimes.com/news/local/la-me-king14aug14,0,5074940.story.

36. See "Martin Luther King, Jr. Multi-Service Ambulatory Care Center," *Wikipedia*, n.d., available at http://en.wikipedia.org/wiki/Martin_Luther_King,_Jr._Multi-Service_Ambulatory_Care_Center (accessed January 22, 2013).

37. Wacquant and Wilson, "The Cost."

38. Carrie Lee, "Safe and Dangerous Places in Los Angeles," AOL Travel, September 9, 2010, available at http://news.travel.aol.com/2010/09/09/safe-and-dangerous-places-in-los-angeles/.

39. Ibid.

40. Barack Obama, *Dreams from My Father: A Story of Race and Inheritance* (New York: Crown, 2007), 277.

41. Gold, "Hoping Peace Moves In," 5.

42. Scott Gold, "Promise and Peril in South Central: The 'Hood as a Tourist Attraction," *Los Angeles Times*, December 5, 2009, available at http://articles.latimes.com/2009/dec/05/local/la-me-southla-tours5–2009dec05.

43. William J. Wilson, *More than Just Race: Being Black and Poor in the Inner City* (New York: Norton, 2009), 46.

CHAPTER 4

1. "Weigh In: Out There, South-Central," previously available at http://www.latimes.com/news/local/la-me-outthere28mar28-gb,0,7325213.graffitiboard?slice=2&limit=10 (accessed November 22, 2011).

2. Patricia Hill Collins, *Black Feminist Thought: Knowledge, Consciousness, and the Politics of Empowerment* (Boston: Unwin Hyman, 1990).

3. James Truslow Adams, *The Epic of America* (1931; repr., New York: Simon, 2001), 15.

4. Robert Longley, "Two Thirds Feel American Dream Harder to Achieve," About .com October 1, 2004, available at http://usgovinfo.about.com/od/moneymatters/a/ daddream.htm.

5. Steve Jones, "Cosby Gives a 'Call Out,'" *USA Today*, May 16, 2006, 10, available at http://www.usatoday.com/life/people/2006–05–16-cosby-main_x .htm?POE=LIFISVA.

6. João H. Costa Vargas, *Catching Hell in the City of Angels: Life and Meanings of Blackness in South Central Los Angeles* (Minneapolis: University of Minnesota Press, 2006).

7. George Lipsitz, *How Racism Takes Place* (Philadelphia: Temple University Press, 2011).

8. Victor Rios, *Punished: Policing the Lives of Black and Latino Boys* (New York: New York University Press, 2011).

9. For in-depth reviews of culture-of-poverty theory, see Bette J. Dickerson, "Centering Studies of African American Single Mothers and Their Families," in *African American Single Mothers*, ed. Bette J. Dickerson, 1–20 (Thousand Oaks, CA: Sage, 1995); and Collins, *Black Feminist Thought*.

10. John Ogbu, *Minority Education and Caste: The American System in Cross-Cultural Perspective* (New York: Academic Press, 1978). See also Angel L. Harris, "Oppositional Culture," in *Encyclopedia of the Life Course and Human Development*, ed. Deborah Carr, Robert Crosnoe, Mary Elizabeth Hughes, and Amy M. Pienta, 329–333 (New York: Macmillan, 2008).

11. Ogbu, *Minority Education and Caste*. See also Signithia Fordham and John U. Ogbu, "Black Students' School Success: Coping with the Burden of 'Acting White,'" *Urban Review* 18 (1986): 176–206.

12. Ogbu, *Minority Education and Caste*.

13. Ibid.

14. Ibid., 10.

15. Ibid.

16. Angela Neal-Barnett, "Being Black: A New Conceptualization of Acting White," in *Forging Links: African American Children Clinical Developmental Perspectives*, ed. Angela M. Neal-Barnett, Josefina M. Contreras, and Kathryn A. Kerns, 67–83 (Westport, CT: Greenwood, 2001).

17. John Ogbu, *Black American Students in an Affluent Suburb: A Study of Academic Disengagement* (Mahwah, NJ: Erlbaum, 2003).

18. Ibid.

19. John McWhorter, *Losing the Race: Self-Sabotage in Black America* (New York: Simon and Schuster, 2000).

20. James S. Coleman, *The Adolescent Society: The Social Life of the Teenager and Its Impact on Education* (New York: Free Press of Glencoe, 1961).

21. Karolyn Tyson, William Darity, Jr., and Domini R. Castellino, "It's Not 'a Black Thing': Understanding the Burden of Acting White and Other Dilemmas of High Achievement," *American Sociological Review* 70, no. 4 (2005): 582–605.

22. Ibid.

23. Ogbu, *Black American Students*. This term has become popular as a way to critique professional Blacks. For example, in a newspaper article with the title "Jesse Jackson

Criticizes 'Acting White' Obama," the author writes that Jackson sharply criticized Barack Obama for "acting like he's white" in what Jackson categories as a "tepid response" to the arrest of six Black juveniles' on attempted-murder charges in Jena, Louisiana. See Stone Martindale, "Jesse Jackson Criticizes 'Acting White' Obama," *M&C*, September 19, 2007, available at http://www.monstersandcritics.com/people/news/article_1357558.php.

24. Claude M. Steele and Joshua Aronson, "Stereotype Threat and the Intellectual Test Performance of African Americans," *Journal of Personality and Social Psychology* 69, no. 5 (1995): 797–811.

25. Ibid.

26. Quoted in Shoshana Polansky, "Routes to Inner-City College Preparatory Success: University of Southern California Neighborhood Academic Initiative," unpublished honors thesis, University of Southern California, 2012, 5.

27. Ibid.

28. Ibid.

29. Steele and Aronson, "Stereotype Threat."

30. Ibid.

31. Ibid.

32. Paul G. Davis, Steven J. Spencer, and Claude M. Steele, "Cleaning the Air: Identity Safety Moderates the Effects of Stereotype Threat on Women's Leadership Aspirations," *Journal of Personality and Social Psychology* 88, no. 2 (2005): 285.

33. Michael Schwalbe, *Rigging the Game: How Inequality Is Reproduced in Everyday Life* (New York: Oxford University Press, 2008), 23.

34. Ibid., 54.

35. Mark K. Smith, "C. Wright Mills: Power, Craftsmanship, and Private Troubles and Public Issues," *Infed*, 2009, available at http://www.infed.org/thinkers/wright _mills.htm.

36. Pierre Bourdieu, *Outline of a Theory of Practice* (Cambridge: Cambridge University Press, 1977).

37. Schwalbe, *Rigging the Game*, 12.

CHAPTER 5

1. Duke Helfand, "U.S. May Force California to Call More School Districts Failures," *Los Angeles Times*, February 17, 2005, available at http://articles.latimes .com/2005/feb/17/local/me-failure17.

2. UCLA/IDEA, "The Crisis in California's School Buildings," 2003, available at http://www.learningace.com/doc/810675/913ee91520f954b9e2a615679176383a/ facilities.

3. "Rand Report Shows California Schools Lag behind Other States on Almost Every Objective Measurement," Rand Corporation, January 3, 2005, available at http:// www.rand.org/news/press/2005/01/03.html. The report did, however, find improvements in students' math achievement.

4. Louis Sahagun and Duke Helfand, "ACLU Sues State over Conditions in Poor Schools," *Los Angeles Times*, May 18, 2000, available at http://articles.latimes .com/2000/may/18/news/mn-31352.

5. Ibid.

6. Jane Gross, "Los Angeles Schools: Hobbled and Hurting," *New York Times*, February 16, 1993, available at http://www.nytimes.com/1993/02/16/us/los-angeles-schools-hobbled-and-hurting.html.

7. See Salt Lake Area Gang Project, "Dressing Down," available at http://updsl.org/divisions/metro_gang_unit/downloads/Dressing%20Down.pdf.

8. According to a report issued by the Illinois State Board of Education, more than 40 million children carry backpacks loaded with books, laptop computers, and other items. More than 7,277 emergency room visits each year result from injuries related to backpacks, and as of 2006, backpack-related injuries were up 330 percent since 1996. Illinois State Board of Education, "Carrying Backpacks: Physical Effects," June 2006, available at http://www.isbe.state.il.us/pdf/Carrying_Backpacks_Physical_Effects.pdf.

9. Complaint filed by plaintiffs in *Williams v. State of California*, available at http://www.decentschools.org/courtdocs/01FirstAmendedComplaint.pdf, p. 9.

10. Jonathon E. Briggs, "District Launches Clean Restroom Hotline," *Los Angeles Times*, January 21, 2000, available at http://articles.latimes.com/2000/jan/21/local/me-56225.

11. Complaint filed by plaintiffs in *Williams v. State of California*, available at http://www.decentschools.org/courtdocs/01FirstAmendedComplaint.pdf, pp. 64–67.

12. Jonathan Kozol, "Still Separate, Still Unequal: America's Educational Apartheid," *Harper's Magazine*, September 1, 2005, 52.

13. UCLA/IDEA, "The Crisis in California's School Buildings."

14. Mitchell Landsberg, "Poorest Schools, Fear, Despair Rule," *Los Angeles Times*, April 26, 2008, available at http://articles.latimes.com/2008/apr/26/local/me-survey26.

15. Harriette Pipes McAdoo, *Black Families* (Thousand Oaks, CA: Sage, 2000), 25.

16. Jeannie Oakes, John Rogers, David Silver, Eileen Homg, and Joanna Goode, *Separate and Unequal 50 Years after* Brown: *California's Racial "Opportunity Gap"* (Los Angeles: UCLA IDEA, 2004).

17. Jonathan Kozol, *Savage Inequalities: Children in America's Schools* (New York: Crown, 1991).

18. Ibid., 2.

19. Ibid., 185.

20. Kozol, "Still Separate, Still Unequal," 42.

21. Also see Alison Crowan, "Schools' Deep-Pocketed Partners," *New York Times*, June 3, 2007, In the Region, p. 13. The author states that in the last decade, a growing number of parents, alumni, and corporations have been donating money to public schools for school equipment and educational supplies that go beyond the usual PTA gifts. The author notes that foundations tend to give money to well-off towns, whose residents are eager and able to support the schools, and to some distressed cities that can attract traditional grants aimed at easing poverty. However, that leaves schools in many districts "muddling along without a strong financial partner."

CHAPTER 6

1. There are a number of stories of gang members helping out the community. In fact, the Black Panthers, on one hand, were really gun-toting, drug-dealing gangsters, but on the other hand, they set up a community-based, nonprofit research, education, and advocacy center dedicated to fostering progressive social change.

2. Mary J. Blige, "You Can Find a Way to Heal," *Parade*, February 4, 2007, 4.

3. Ibid.

4. Patricia J. Williams, *The Alchemy of Race and Rights: Diary of a Law Professor* (Cambridge, MA: Harvard University Press, 1992), 1.

5. Joe Mathews, Erika Hayasaki, and Duke Helfand, "School Called 'Out of Control': Teachers and Students at Washington Prep High Describe Crime, Sex Acts, Drug Use on Campus," *Los Angeles Times*, November 21, 2002, available at http://articles.latimes.com/2002/nov/21/local/me-prep21_.

6. Claudio Sanchez, "Los Angeles School Struggles to Leave Violence Behind," *NPR*, May 10, 2006, available at http://www.npr.org/templates/story/story.php?storyId=5395417.

7. Earl Ofari Hutchinson, "Los Angeles School Brawls Expose Black-Latino Tension," *Pacific News Service*, April 27, 2005, available at http://news.newamericamedia.org/news/view_article.html?article_id=00c83b0739520c4f380469df2c520743. See also Farai Chideya and Mandalit del Barco, "Racial Tension at Los Angeles High School," *NPR*, May 16, 2005, available at http://www.npr.org/templates/story/story.php?storyId=4653328.

8. Hutchinson, "Los Angeles School Brawls."

9. Ibid.

10. Quoted in Jane Gross, "Los Angeles Schools: Hobbled and Hurting," *New York Times*, February 16, 1993, available at http://www.nytimes.com/1993/02/16/us/los-angeles-schools-hobbled-and-hurting.html.

11. Joe Matthews, "Metal Detectors and a Search for Peace of Mind," *Los Angeles Times*, May 30, 2000, B2.

12. Joe Mathews, "Metal Detectors and a Search for Peace of Mind," *Los Angeles Times*, May 30, 2001, available at http://articles.latimes.com/2001/may/30/local/me-4196.

13. John Devine, *Maximum Security: The Culture of Violence in Inner-City Schools* (Chicago: University of Chicago Press, 1996), 1.

14. Ibid., 236.

15. ChefMikeyD, "Inner City Schools," CollegeNet, January 14, 2007, available at http://www.collegenet.com/elect/app/app?service=external/Forum&sp=1503#2389.

16. Mitchell Landsberg, "Schools with High Dropout Rates Listed," *Los Angeles Times*, February 21, 2008, available at http://articles.latimes.com/2008/feb/21/local/me-dropout21.

17. Paul Willis has argued, "What kind of bourgeoisie is it that does not in some way believe its own legitimation? That would be the denial of themselves." Quoted in Jay MacLeod, *Ain't No Makin' It: Aspirations and Attainment in a Low-Income Neighborhood*, 3rd ed. (Norwood, MA: Westwood Press, 2009), 264.

18. Ibid.

19. Ibid., 3.

20. Marlene Ricker, "Inner-City Schools: How to Keep the Elite," UAB Publications, 2005, available at http://main.uab.edu/show.asp?durki=91334.

21. Migdia Chinea, "Battle-Scarred 'Sub' in L.A. Barrios Speaks Out," *WND Commentary*, November 16, 2007, available at http://www.wnd.com/news/article.asp?ARTICLE_ID=58713.

22. For discussions of inner-city kids' school problems, see Elijah Anderson, *Codes of the Street: Decency, Violence, and the Moral Life of the Inner City* (New York: Norton, 1999); Cristina Rathbone, *On the Outside Looking In: A Year in an Inner-City High School* (New York: Atlantic Monthly Press, 1998); David Simon and Edwards Burns, *The Corner: A Year in the Life of an Inner-City Neighborhood* (New York: Broadway Books, 1997); and Laura Preble, "Classroom Overcrowding: It's Not Just a Numbers Game," *TeachHUB*, n.d., available at http://www.teachhub.com/classroom-overcrowding (accessed January 22, 2013).

23. See Heitor Villa-Lobos's biography in Oscar Thompson, ed., *The International Cyclopedia of Music and Musicians* (New York: Dodd, Mead, 1938), 2311.

24. Michael Schwalbe, *Rigging the Game: How Inequality Is Reproduced in Everyday Life* (New York: Oxford University Press, 2008), 107.

25. Melissa A. Milkie and Catharine H. Warner, "Classroom Learning Environments and the Mental Health of First Grade Children," *Journal of Health and Social Behavior* 52, no. 1 (2011): 4–22.

26. Daniel J. Losen, *Discipline Policies, Successful School, and Racial Justice* (Boulder, CO: National Education Policy Center, 2011).

27. Milkie and Warner, "Classroom Learning Environments," 5.

28. Kathy, e-mail message to author, May 28, 2011.

29. Max, e-mail message to author, May 28, 2011.

30. Jason, e-mail message to author, May 28, 2011.

31. MacLeod, *Ain't No Makin' It*. The author conducted these interviews years before President Obama became the first African American to become president. Note, however, that Obama's path to the presidency was paved by a strong middle-class background and a Harvard education. Most poor kids will not have that kind of class background. Their chances of even finding a living-wage job are limited because they are minorities and because they are poor.

32. See Ed Wonk, "Los Angeles' Combat High School," *Education Wonks*, May 13, 2008, available at http://educationwonk.blogspot.com/2008/05/los-angeles-combat-high-school.html.

33. Samuel Bowles and Herbert Gintis, *Schooling in Capitalist America: Educational Reform and the Contradictions of Economic Life* (New York: Basic Books, 1977).

34. Ibid.; John Ogbu, *Minority Status, Oppositional Culture, and Schooling* (New York: Taylor and Francis, 2008).

35. See John McWhorter, *Losing the Race: Self-Sabotage in Black America* (New York: Harper Perennial, 2001).

36. Jonathan Kozol, *Savage Inequalities: Children in America's Schools* (New York: Crown, 1991).

CHAPTER 7

1. Margaret Beale Spencer, "Resiliency and Fragility Factor Associated with the Contextual Experiences of Low-Resource Urban African-American Male Youth and Families," in *Does It Take a Village? Community Effects on Children, Adolescents, and Families*, ed. Alan Booth and Ann C. Crouter (New York: Psychology Press, 2000), 53.

2. The Census Bureau reports that occupations like those of the kids' families, such as cleaning, personal and health care service, construction, and fast-food service, earn

on average $21,000 to $40,000 a year. Alemayehu Bishaw and Jessica Semega, *Income, Earnings, and Poverty Data from the 2007 American Community Survey* (Washington, DC: U.S. Government Printing Office, 2008), available at http://www.census.gov/prod/2008pubs/acs-09.pdf.

3. For an interesting take on bats as weapons, see *Big Stick Combat Blog* at http://bigstickcombat.wordpress.com/tag/real-weapons.

4. According to *USA Today*, about two million families nationwide face a similarly gut-wrenching risk of deportation because the children are U.S.-born citizens but at least one parent is an illegal immigrant. See Wendy Koch, "'Mixed Status' Tears Apart Families," *USA Today*, April 25, 2006, available at http://usatoday30.usatoday.com/news/nation/2006-04-25-mixed-status_x.htm.

5. Randy Kennedy, "Celebrating Forefather of Graffiti," *New York Times*, July 22, 2011, available at http://www.nytimes.com/2011/07/23/arts/design/early-graffiti-artist-taki-183-still-lives.html?_r=0.

6. Stanley Tookie Williams III (December 29, 1953–December 13, 2005) was a convicted murderer and an early leader of the Crips, a notorious American street gang that formed in South Central Los Angeles in 1971. That he helped form the Crips was his greatest regret. Behind bars he became a leading advocate for the end of gang violence. He wrote nine books and has been nominated several times for the Nobel Peace Prize. In December 2005, he was executed. See Jennifer Warren and Maura Dolan, "Tookie Williams Is Executed," *Los Angeles Times*, December 13, 2005, available at http://www.latimes.com/news/local/la-me-execution13dec13,0,799154.story.

7. Bruce H. Rankin and James M. Quane, "Neighborhood Poverty and the Social Isolation of Inner-City African American Families," *Social Forces* 79, no. 1 (2000): 140.

8. George L. Kelling and James Q. Wilson, "Broken Windows: The Police and Neighborhood Safety," *The Atlantic*, March 1982, available at http://www.theatlantic.com/magazine/archive/1982/03/broken-windows/4465/.

9. Shelley E. Taylor, Rena L. Repetti, and Teresa Seeman, "Health Psychology: What Is an Unhealthy Environment and How Does It Get under the Skin?" *Annual Review of Psychology* 48 (1997): 411.

10. John Ogbu, *The Next Generation: An Ethnography of Education in an Urban Neighborhood* (New York: Academic Press, 1974).

11. Herbert J. Gans, *The War against the Poor: The Underclass and Antipoverty Policy* (New York: Basic Books, 1992).

12. Ray Bradbury, *Something Wicked This Way Comes* (New York: Avon Books, 1962).

CHAPTER 8

1. Post by "Mossomo," City-Data.com, May 12, 2009, available at http://www.city-data.com/forum/politics-other-controversies/646104-why-do-inner-city-residents-allow-2.html#ixzz1OiRzbscB.

2. For example, see Leslie Sykes, "Vigil Held for USC Student Killed," *KABC*, September 18, 2008, available at http://abclocal.go.com/kabc/story?section=news/local/los_angeles&id=6399009.

3. Anselm Strauss, *Images of the American City* (New Brunswick, NJ: Transaction, 1976), 66.

4. Peter Orleans, "Differential Cognition of Urban Residents: Effects of Social Scale on Mapping," in *Image and Environment: Cognitive Mapping and Spatial Behavior*, ed. Roger Downs and David Stea (New Brunswick, NJ: Transaction, 2005), 128.

5. Jay MacLeod, *Ain't No Makin' It: Aspirations and Attainment in a Low-Income Neighborhood*, 3rd ed. (Norwood, MA: Westwood Press, 2009); João H. Costa Vargas, *Catching Hell in the City of Angels: Life and Meanings of Blackness in South Central Los Angeles* (Minneapolis: University of Minnesota Press, 2006). See also Elaine Bell Kaplan, *Not Our Kind of Girl: Unraveling the Myth of Black Teenage Motherhood* (Berkeley: University of California Press, 1999).

CHAPTER 9

1. William Madson, "Anxiety and Witchcraft in Mexican-American Acculturation," *Anthropological Quarterly* 39, no. 2 (1966): 110–127.

2. Luis H. Zayas, Rebecca J. Lester, Leopoldo J. Cabassa, and Lisa R. Fortuna, "Why Do So Many Latina Teenagers Attempt Suicide? A Conceptual Model for Research," *American Journal of Orthopsychiatry* 75, no. 2 (2005): 275–287.

3. Ibid., 279.

4. Ibid.

5. Andreana T. Jezzini, Cynthia E. Guzmán, and Lisa Grayshield, "Examining the Gender Role Concept of *Marianismo* and Its Relation to Acculturation in Mexican-American College Women," 2008, available at http://counselingoutfitters.com/vistas/vistas08/Jezzini.htm.

6. Carol Stack, *All Our Kin* (New York: Harper and Row, 1974).

7. William Golding, *Lord of the Flies* (London: Faber and Faber, 1954).

CHAPTER 10

1. Jim Hubbard, "About," Shooting Back, available at http://shootingback.net/ (accessed January 7, 2012).

2. Manuel Pastor, personal communication with author, January 19, 2012.

3. Hubbard, "About."

4. Tennessee Advisory Commission on Intergovernmental Relations, "Do K–12 School Facilities Affect Education Outcomes?" January 2003, available at http://www.state.tn.us/tacir/PDF_FILES/Education/SchFac.pdf.

5. Mitchell Landsberg, "In Poorest Schools, Fear, Despair Rule," *Los Angeles Times*, April 26, 2008, available at http://articles.latimes.com/2008/apr/26/local/me-survey26.

6. Vincent, e-mail message to author, July 10, 2012.

7. In February 2012, Trayvon Martin, a seventeen-year-old Black youth, was shot to death by George Zimmerman, a "multiracial" neighborhood watch volunteer for a gated community where Martin was staying and where the shooting took place. Martin was wearing a hooded sweatshirt that some people believe may have led Zimmerman to describe him on his 911 phone call before he shot Martin as a "real suspicious guy" who was "cutting in between houses" and "walking very leisurely for the [rainy] weather." The police later determined that Martin was coming home from a 7-Eleven store carrying Skittles and a can of iced tea.

8. In the literature on the Black community, this phenomenon is called "Black flight." "White flight" is the term used for the movement of White families from urban areas to the suburbs—for example, in Chicago and Detroit in the 1960s and 1970s. See, for example, Wiliam Juluis Wilson, *More than Just Race: Being Black and Poor in the Inner City* (New York: W. W. Norton, 2010); and Rachael A. Woldoff, *White Flight/ Black Flight: The Dynamics of Racial Change in an American Neighborhood* (Ithaca, NY: Cornell University Press, 2011).

9. Manuel Pastor, personal communication with author, January 19, 2012.

10. Michael Schwalbe, *Rigging the Game: How Inequality is Reproduced in Everyday Life* (New York: Oxford University Press, 2008).

11. Katherine Call, "The Implications of Helplessness for Possible Selves," in *Adolescents, Work and Family: An Intergenerational Development Analysis*, ed. Jaylen T. Mortimer and Michael D. Finch (Thousand Oaks, CA: Sage, 1996), 63–96.

12. Elise Boulding, "The Nurture of Adults by Children in Family Settings," in *Research in the Interweave of Social Roles: Women and Men*, ed. Helena Z. Lopata (Greenwich, CT: JAI Press, 1980), 167–189.

13. See, for example, T. W. Ward, *Gangsters without Borders: An Ethnography of a Salvadoran Street Gang* (New York: Oxford University Press, 2013). Ward argues that "gangs exaggerate or amplify the negative characterisitics of human aggression, violence, distrust, exploitation, cynicism, and sexism, which are the by products of impoverished lives in urban ghettos, where the dog-eat-dog survival street code thrives" (2).

14. Boulding, "The Nurture of Adults by Children in Family Settings."

15. Hillary Rodham Clinton, *It Takes a Village: And Other Lessons Children Teach Us* (New York: Touchstone, 1996), 7.

16. Robert J. Sampson, "How Do Communities Undergird or Undermine Human Development? Relevant Contexts and Social Mechanisms," in *Does It Take a Village? Community Effects on Children, Adolescents, and Families*, ed. Alan Booth and Ann C. Crouter (New York: Psychology Press, 2000), 12.

17. Research findings suggest that gangs appear to shield youth from unsatisfactory home environments and provide a means of survival in neighborhoods with high levels of criminal and gang activity. For these youth, peer (i.e., not losing friends) and interpersonal (i.e., a sense of belonging or status) factors also made gang membership appealing. Stanley J. Huey, Dawn D. McDaniel, Caitlin A. Smith, and James P. Griffin, Jr., "Gang-Involved, African American Youth: An Overview," unpublished manuscript, July 1, 2010.

18. Erik Erikson, *Identity: Youth and Crisis* (New York: Norton, 1968), 102.

19. The American Civil Liberties Union (ACLU) of Southern California is suing the city of Glendale, administrators at Hoover High School, and three law enforcement agencies over a case of racial profiling. That is how the ACLU describes what happened on a September day at Hoover High in 2010. It claims that fifty-six Latino students were rounded up and then searched and interrogated by police. The students were questioned about gang affiliations, tattoos, and scars. Glendale school officials deny the racial profiling charge. See "ACLU/SC Sues over Questioning of Latino Students at Glendale's Hoover High School," *OurWeekly*, October 14, 2011, available at http://www.our weekly.com/los-angeles/aclusc-sues-over-questioning-latino-students-glendale's-hoover -high-school. It may be that school officals did not understand that they were treating

these kids as ghetto thugs. But the kids in my study would think so. This event supports the point that the kids make throughout this book—that inner-city kids are treated like criminals.

20. Tim Burton, *The Melancholy Death of Oyster Boy and Other Stories* (New York: HarperCollins, 1997), 9.

21. Susan J. Popkin, Gregory Acs, and Robin Smith, "The Urban Institute's Program on Neighborhoods and Youth Development: Understanding How Place Matters for Kids," 2009, available at http://www.urban.org/UploadedPDF/411974 _place_matters.pdf.

22. See Celeste Fremon, *G-Dog and the Homeboys: Father Greg Boyle and the Gangs of East Los Angeles* (Albuquerque: University of New Mexico Press, 2008). Also see Nikki Jones, *Between Good and Ghetto: African American Girls and Inner-City Violence* (New Brunswick, NJ: Rutgers University Press, 2009).

Index

Supreme Court, U.S., 31
Sureños gang, 32
suspensions, 73–74, 83
symbolic interactionism, 23

tagging, *104*, 104–106
"Take the A Train" (Ellington and Strayhorn), 13
Tanana (student), *74*
Taylor (USC volunteer at NAI), 83–84
teachers: good and bad, 80–81; on problems with students, 79; as reinforcing institutional inequality, 157; substitutes, 35, 56, 80, 84; as uninterested in teaching, 74–75, *75*, *76*, 83–85, 155, 157, 159, 161; Wynette on, 70–73, *72*
teenage mothers, 15
Tennessee Advisory Commission, 152
Terry (USC student from South Central), 6–7, 24
Theresa (USC student), 4–5, 35, 96
Thomas (NAI student), 91–92, 97–99
Thomas, W. I., 23
Thomas-Barrios, Kim, 15, 53–54, 62
Tierney, William, 47
tracking, 47
travel guides, 38
Tyson, Karolyn, 46

union work, 33, 34
unwed mothers, 43
UPI (United Press International) photography program, 151–152
urban sprawl, 29
USC (University of Southern California), 4–7, 31, 32, 47, 155, *156*, *157*

Vargas, João Helion Costa, 43, 123

Victor (USC student from South Central), 6–7, 24
Vincent (USC student), 153–154

Wacquant, Loïc, 34, 35, 38
Wallerstein, Nina, 18
Walmart, 37
Wang, Caroline, 17, 20
Warner, Catharine, 83
Washington Prep High School, 73, 77
Watts Riots, 32
West Adams, 31
White engineering students and stereotype threat, 48
"White flight," 185n8
Whiting, Marge, 56–57
Willard after-school center, 7, 47, 54–57
Williams, Patricia, 71
Williams, Tookie, 106, 183n6
Willis, Paul, 181n17
Wilson, James Q., 107
Wilson, William J., 34, 35, 38, 39
Winfield, Paul, 31
Winfrey, Oprah, 42
witchcraft, 131–132
women: Latinas, 138–140; and stereotype threat, 48; teenage mothers, 15; unwed mothers, 43
wrecked cars, *96*, 96–97, *97*
Wynette (NAI student), 3, 80; on bad teachers, 71–73, *72*, 155, 160; coping with problems, 86; on disruption of frequent moves, 69–70; and protection by gang members, 70–71, 149; wearing latest fashions, 119, *120*

Zayas, Luis, 138
Zimmerman, George, 154, 184n7 (ch. 10)

Elaine Bell Kaplan is Associate Professor in the Department of Sociology at the University of Southern California and author of *Not Our Kind of Girl: Unraveling the Myths of Black Teenage Motherhood.*